D1650381

All-Age
Worship

Text copyright © Lucy Moore 2010
The author asserts the moral right
to be identified as the author of this work

Published by
The Bible Reading Fellowship
15 The Chambers, Vineyard
Abingdon OX14 3FE
United Kingdom
Tel: +44 (0)1865 319700
Email: enquiries@brf.org.uk
Website: www.brf.org.uk
BRF is a Registered Charity

ISBN 978 1 84101 432 6

First published 2010
Reprinted 2011
10 9 8 7 6 5 4 3 2 1
All rights reserved

Acknowledgments
Unless otherwise stated, scripture quotations are taken from the Holy Bible, New International
Version, copyright © 1973, 1978, 1984 by International Bible Society, are used by permission
of Hodder & Stoughton Publishers, a member of the Hachette Livre UK Group. All rights
reserved. 'NIV' is a registered trademark of International Bible Society. UK trademark number
1448790.

Scriptures quoted from the Contemporary English Version published by The Bible Societies/
HarperCollins Publishers copyright © American Bible Society 1991, 1992, 1995, used with
permission.

A catalogue record for this book is available from the British Library

Printed in Singapore by Craft Print International Ltd

All-Age
Worship

Lucy Moore

— * —

For Lesley, John and Emily Hudson, and Gill, Pete, Hannah,
Richard and Esther Jowett, who have given our family
a wonderful experience of unconditional love
over so many years.

— * —

Acknowledgments

With thanks especially to Martyn Payne and Paul Moore for their wise contributions, those who have kindly allowed their churches to be mentioned in this book, Chris Rees, Marcus Bull and other members of the Intergenerational Church Forum and Naomi Starkey.

Contents

*

Introduction

'Noooooo!'

The prospect of all-age worship can easily produce a cry of anguish from... well, from so many people.

'Is it Junior Church this week?' ask the children. 'No, it's the first week of the month—we're together today!' declares their leader gleefully, to be met by eight-year-old sagging shoulders, grumbles and pouts.

'All-age worship again!' sighs the minister, desperately short of time to prepare anything other than a standard liturgy-based service rather than the moving and life-changing worship experience she has read about, using a ten-foot-high, all-singing, all-dancing, glow-in-the-dark visual aid made from recycled eggboxes.

'Oh. The children are in, are they?' comes the less-than-enthusiastic response from the 40-something single person, echoed by the weary father of three who was hoping for half an hour of peace and quiet and now can only look forward to an hour of embarrassment and crowd control.

It's time to be real. It's time to admit that worship with all ages present is easy to do appallingly and difficult to do well. It's time to acknowledge that it takes a huge amount of grace from every participant. But it's also time to admit that a church that unthinkingly packs off any subgroup, old or young, to worship and learn in another space every week could well be as daft as a person merrily cutting off his own leg. It's as ridiculous as that.

A great deal has been written about all-age worship. There are many suggested service outlines for inclusive church services. So what's special about this book?

This book is for those who sense that worshipping God together is probably a good thing, but are nervous of trying to lead their church towards that vision. It tries to stay grounded in reality. It doesn't zoom off into glorious impracticalities involving rotating stages, 90 hours of preparation and prayer equipment that costs a tenner a head. It takes account of the rich variety of church life in all its stubbornness, selfishness, wistfulness and bewilderment. It acknowledges that we don't live in a perfect world and that no one person—certainly not I—has all the answers. It also recognises that you are the expert for the ways in which your church can best worship God, and anything that is suggested within these pages needs to be sifted through your own opinion and adapted for your own local setting.

Chapter 1 asks if church should be all-age when it is so difficult to achieve. Chapter 2 stands back to look at what church worship is about, as a background to considering all-age worship more specifically. Chapter 3 considers the key part that relationship has to play in our church services, while Chapter 4 suggests some rules of thumb for running all-age services. Chapter 5 acknowledges that this is a terrifying prospect for some people and is about helping a congregation cope with change, and Chapter 6 provides some practical details and service examples. It's a big-picture overview of why we might try to do all-age worship, with hands-on detail to show that it isn't just pie in the sky.

What I'm *not* trying to do is to supply another set of *Super All-Age Services for Septuagesima* or suggest *Ten Handy Hints for Praying Together Without Tears*. This book isn't a tick list of *Five Ways To Make Your Worship Mean Something To Everyone* or *1000 Easy Talks for the Whole Family*.

No, this book tries to bring together some of the current bigger thinking about why it's good to worship together. We need to understand why we're not taking the easier 'traditional' option of segregation, before we work out the hows and whats. But the hows and whats are important, so later chapters concentrate on principles and practical ideas for worshipping together.

The book also concentrates on the aspect of worship that is the gathered community of Christians coming together to praise God, meet him and learn about him—what we traditionally see as 'a church service'. This book hasn't got space to explore the bigger idea of what church is, or how worship happens in every part of life: it will concentrate on why we might worship corporately, and what we might do in that time together.

Is it time to confess that although this book concentrates on 'all-age' worship, I hate the term? I find it very misleading but I can't think of an alternative that doesn't sound offensive to the rest of church—'everybody church'; 'church for anyone'; 'whole church'? Surely all church should always be for anyone? The reason for my problem with 'all-age' church is that, although we know it's emphasising a particular aspect of church, it assumes that the only significant difference between people is their age. 'Intergenerational worship' as a term has the same problem, and as for 'family service'—with the history of the family service in the Anglican Church and the tensions surrounding what people assume we mean when we talk about 'family'—I run a mile from it. I can only hope that 'all-age' is one of those terms that will see us through a period of change in the church and, in 50 years, will be laughably quaint and redundant. As soon as we call worship 'all-age', we divide people solely by the number of years they have been alive, not by their depth of spirituality, how long they have been a Christian, how they prefer to learn, what their strengths are, how deeply committed to Christ they are, or any other definition that tries to grasp the happy diversity of the people whom Christ has called to follow him. So in this book we'll step back and start to look at the people in our churches in other ways than by age: perhaps we'll be surprised.

All-age questions challenge the very heart of what churches are doing. They encourage us to re-evaluate what we do and why we do it. At this time of new opportunities for being church in different ways, let's keep asking, 'How can we be the best churches that we possibly can?'

In recent years, BRF's *Barnabas* children's team has been thinking through the issues around all-age worship and has been leading sessions for church groups across the country on the subject, in many different settings and across the denominations. It began as a common interest and has developed into a passion. We have shared the experience of members of the Intergenerational Forum, which started life under the leadership of CPAS (Church Pastoral Aid Society) and has continued independently. Apart from the invaluable insights gained from other team members and the people we have worked with at these events, most of my own experience in this area has come through our local parish work with Messy Church.

I've written about Messy Church more fully elsewhere, but, in brief: in 2004 a group of children's leaders in our Anglican church near Portsmouth decided that if we really wanted to make an impact on the lives of children, the most effective and far-reaching way was to try to work with the whole family unit, not with children in isolation from the people who have most influence on them—those who are bringing them up. We devised a pattern of church centred around the needs and wants of families who find it hard to belong to traditional Sunday church. So the timing, the frequency, the activities and length of sessions and the application of the Bible all come from the needs of this group of people. The emphasis is on a relaxed welcome, a choice of hands-on creative activities, some celebration time to bring all our worship before God and enjoy story, song and prayer together, and eating together at tables.

As Messy Church became established and started developing, not just in our own church but across the UK and beyond, thanks to the promotion by Fresh Expressions and the efforts of BRF's *Barnabas* ministry team, it became increasingly apparent that encouraging ages and generations to worship together appeals to people in and outside church and seems to speak of God's longing for wholeness in a divided world. So, despite the temptations we face to reduce it to a 'children's church' or to water down the celebration and other activities to a lowest common denominator, we keep on struggling to respond to the needs and aspirations of the whole age range, not just those of children. It is difficult to keep focused on being genuinely all-age. It's hard to break away from the traditional view that any event with children present is purely and simply a children's event. It's a challenge to worship and learn alongside children rather than turning the processes into a one-way flow in which 'we have the answers and you need to learn from us'. There's so much left to find out, but as we gradually draw together the lessons we are learning from the different Messy Churches across the country, in their very different social situations, perhaps the wider church can benefit from them.

You can read more about the Messy Church journey in the books *Messy Church* and *Messy Church 2*, as well as on the website (www.messychurch.org.uk), where you can also find information about Messy Fiesta days. These days give opportunities for Messy Church leaders and potential leaders to find out more about this way of being church and to share ideas about the way forward.

Through the *Barnabas* children's team network and through our links with similarly-minded colleagues in different denominations, we are learning something about God's love of wholeness, about the paradox of bringing together as many differences as possible in order to become as much like him as possible, about the joy of working with messily imperfect situations, and about a growth to maturity that depends on being together rather than separated. For some people, this is self-evident and they will need to read no further. For me, and for many people I've met over the last few years, it is the sort of epiphany that lights up a whole new outlook on how we could be church. As we set out to look at these huge and exciting questions, here is a manifesto for all-age church, a 'working document' that underpins our thinking. It is by no means perfect and complete but it helps to summarise something of our passion for being church for all ages.

A manifesto for all-age church

We believe in God who created us for him and for each other.

We believe in Jesus who welcomes young and old without exception.

We believe in the Holy Spirit who transforms the life of all believers, young and old.

We believe in meeting God most intimately in the lives of those who are different from ourselves.

We believe in a church which reflects God, the three in one.

We believe we grow closer to Jesus as his disciples when we:

- worship God in a variety of ways, both familiar and different.
- worship in community as well as individually.
- worship in a way that encourages everyone to participate.
- worship in a way that both enriches and is enriched by our everyday life.
- worship God with all that we are.

Copyright issues

CCLI (Christian Copyright Licensing International) can give churches copyright cover for reproducing song words, playing films and recorded music and much more, and help you to make sure you're legal as you do so. All the information and advice is available on their website: www.ccli.co.uk.

*

– Chapter 1 –

Should church be all-age?

An all-age picture

The icon of the Trinity by Andre Rublev has been used by many fresh expressions of church in the last few years, so much so that it seems almost clichéd in some circles. In case you, like me, haven't come across it until recently, this is what it looks like: a trio of strangely similar yet different figures, in robes, sitting around three sides of a table on which is a cup and a plate of bread. Their robes blend colours of earthy browns, growing greens, diaphanous gold and heavenly blues. One of the three is gesturing towards the cup. They seem to be still, yet oddly full of action under the surface: the icon has a very dynamic quality. You feel that at any minute they might start to eat, begin an animated conversation, get up and dance or go and fetch someone else to fill in the empty space.

In the background are three landscapes—a city, a rocky mountain and some trees. Perhaps these are Abraham and Sarah's three visitors at the oaks at Mamre, described in Genesis 18. Perhaps they are simply the three persons of the Trinity sitting around a heavenly feast. Perhaps it is a picture of what church could be like at its best—glorying in intimate fellowship but open and welcoming to outsiders; full of people who have plenty in common but remain distinct from each other; a community that draws from the past but looks to what is yet to come; diverse but unified, echoing in its very nature a God who is diverse yet unified, three in one.

If this is a picture of what Christian community could be, it is both beautiful and disturbing—disturbing because it's very hard for many of us to see either ourselves as individuals or our church communities in their painful, selfish, petty, struggling realities reflected in this tranquil icon. The ideal is so far from the reality. The picture would be unbalanced without any one of the three characters, and without the unseen observer who at the moment takes up the fourth place—the outsider welcomed in. As a parable of the Church, it speaks of interdependency, the enjoyment of being together. It relishes the differences between the members, seeing those differences not as something that creates conflict and disharmony but as something that is essential for the bigger picture—complementary, not jarring. Also, of course, it invites us to think about the person not yet in the picture, the watcher on the outside, the person on the edge who is waiting to be called to the table.

On their own the colours are beautiful enough, but together they gain significance by their very differences. The icon is a challenge and a vision of what might be.

Speaking of colours, it's time for some light relief. Here's a story to introduce the idea of diversity.

The rainbow that nearly wasn't

God rubbed his hands in glee. The terrible flood was over! There were the animals coming out of the ark—trotting, wobbling, slithering, flying or trundling down on to the mountaintop—and there were Noah and his family building the altar to say 'thank you' for their rescue. God had a lovely surprise ready for them, something that would finish off their adventure with a beautiful ending, to be remembered for thousands of years to come.

'Oh, colours!' called God. 'It's your big moment!'

The gorgeous colours appeared around God's throne, but God could see that something wasn't right. Orange was scowling. Red was grumpy. Blue was kicking the floor. Green was in a strop. Yellow had turned his back on everyone else and Purple seemed about to burst into tears.

'What in heaven is going on?' asked God.

The first colour to speak was Red.

'You said you wanted to put a bow in the sky,' she said. 'Well, I think it should be red. Just red. Nothing but red. Don't mess about with this bunch of losers. Make it red.'

'Why?' asked God.

'Red is the boss of the colours. People really notice red. Red is hot and bright—the colour for fire and blood and traffic signs. If you want this bow to be noticed, you need it to be red.'

'I see,' murmured God.

'No! No! No! No!' squeaked Yellow. 'Your bow should be a beautiful yellow colour, Lord! Make it as yellow as the sunshine! As yellow as bananas! Make it bright and cheerful and shiny as me! Make it just yellow!'

'You are very beautiful,' agreed God.

'But you're not as important as me!' Purple said pompously. 'Look! It's obvious the bow should be purple. Purple is the colour of emperors and kings. Purple is the sign of the most important. If you want power, pick pure purple.'

'I do like purple,' he said.

'But you don't want a poxy purple bow!' shouted Green.

'Wheee! Look at me! Imagine a green bow in the sky! Now that would be really wow! Green is so zingy! So fizzy! So fresh! Like a bottle of green limeade sprayed across the sky. Don't mix me up with these other dull colours—make your bow green!'

'Oh please,' called Orange. 'It's so obvious that orange is the colour you want. Orange like the sunrise. Orange is fruity and juicy and ripe! Make your bow orange, Lord!'

'You are so, like, unhip, man,' said Blue. 'It is so, like, obvious that God's bow should be blue. Blue as the sea and sky, blue like rhythm 'n' blues. Blue like Sonic the Hedgehog blue. Blue is like the coolest colour in your box, Lord. I just know you're going to make your bow blue blue blue.'

Instantly all the colours started shouting at each other.

'Blue is boring!'

'Red is rubbish!'

'Purple's pathetic!'

'Yellow is so last year!'

'Green is gross!'

'Orange sucks!'

'Make your bow red! Blue! Yellow! Orange! Green! Purple!'

God raised one hand and spoke in a voice that no one could disobey. 'Be quiet.'

When the colours had settled down, trembling, God smiled at them.

'You are all just what I want you to be. Each of you does a different job. Without you, I couldn't do this most important job of all. I need to give my people a sign of my promise. I need them to know it is a perfect promise that will never be broken. I need them to know that it is for *all* people of *all* ages from *all* countries for *all* times. And so, my dear dear colours, I need you all. Please, just for a moment, look at each other through my eyes.'

The colours looked at each other and, now that they were looking through God's eyes, they saw how beautiful each of the others was. With a big smile, they stood together and together counted, 'Three, two, one...' Down below, the humans and animals looked up in wonder, for there, between heaven and earth, shone a radiant multicoloured rainbow. Red, orange, yellow, green, blue, purple. All different. All beautiful. All together.

Add some coloured flags, a set of ribbons in rainbow colours, a different action for the audience to do at the mention of each colour's name and you have a story to appeal to your visual learners, your auditory learners and your kinaesthetic ones (people who learn best by seeing, listening and being active respectively) all at the same time, as well as a story that can be taken at several different levels. It could be a good learning experience for people with all these learning styles— but more of that later.

For the moment, it is obvious to any listener or reader of that story that it would be completely inappropriate of God to omit a colour from the rainbow or to give pre-eminence to any one colour just because it thinks it is the most important. Yet it takes the supernatural effort of 'looking at each other through God's eyes' to reach the point where they can all accept each other as equal partners in the job they have to do. We shouldn't underestimate the supernatural grace needed to be an all-age church. It is never going to be the easy option, but that doesn't stop it being the best option—perhaps the only option for a church called to be Jesus' ambassadors in the world.

Reflecting the diversity of God

As Jesus' ambassadors, we need to reflect the fullness of our creating, redeeming and sustaining God. The Rublev icon gives us a picture of diversity in unity—perhaps a family at its best, laughing around a table, a community where the outsider is graciously and generously welcomed. This is a place where everyone can be themselves—indeed, needs to be themselves or the bigger picture is thrown out of kilter—a place where every person is welcome, regardless of age. Here, the kaleidoscopic mix of differences reflects the glorious God we worship and brings us closer to him and to each other.

A community of differences

In church, we have one of the few opportunities in Western society to be a real all-age community, a community where cerebral learning (head learning) is only one aspect of lifelong maturing. In church, people of all sorts can come together and be vulnerable together and grow together. It's a place where the power balance is turned upside down and the nobodies have as much clout as the somebodies—not because everybody is the same, but because everybody is needed for their differences.

Our diversity is something to celebrate. We are gloriously different—and not just in age.

- We learn in different ways.
- We have different personalities.
- We have different intellectual abilities.

- We have different verbal/reading abilities.
- We have different physical abilities.
- We have different world experiences.
- We have different spiritual experiences.
- We have different emotional experiences.
- We have different powers of concentration.
- We come from different cultures and home backgrounds.

What else could you add to this list?

So why, in church, do we traditionally focus on the difference in age? Why do we send children and teenagers out of the main body of the worshipping community? Why don't we segregate people according to their reading age or their learning preference, their concentration span, what sort of chair they like to sit on, their preferred newspaper, their spiritual maturity, their emotional maturity or their open or closed personality? As soon as we start listing all the glorious differences between us, it becomes ridiculous to try to hive just one subsection off to worship or learn in isolation. Yet children are the one subgroup that many churches deliberately and systematically exclude from the worshipping body of the church.

The Revd Eric Kyte, an Anglican vicar in Yorkshire and supporter of the Intergenerational Forum, tells of an all-age service that turned upside down his expectations about what would appeal to whom.

We did an all-age service where the theme was the Sower. The parable was enacted by throwing bean seed over the congregation and the 'Word' was 'plant the seed and bring it back next time'. The idea being, many would forget, some wouldn't hear, etc.—you get the picture. The following month, as it was August, there were no children present but all the old ladies turned up with bean plants!

Let's not think that we can lump people of a certain age bracket together and assume that they all need the same thing.

A thought-provoking activity to try to illustrate these assumptions involves printing out the personality profiles from the Appendix (see pages 174–180) on to separate cards. Distribute the cards so that everyone has one. Then ask people to imagine they are the character described on their card and to make decisions accordingly. Depending on your group, you might ask them to move about the room as described below, or you might invite them simply to talk about the different aspects in character, either in small groups or gathered together.

Say:

I'm going to call out some aspects of our church life. I'd like you to go and stand on an imaginary line down the middle of the room. Stand at this end if your character strongly agrees with the issue, and stand at the other end if your character strongly disagrees. Of course, you might pick a middle-of-the-road position in the middle of the line. So stand where you need to be...

- if you can read all the song words without an effort.
- if you've been a Christian long enough to know it isn't all fun and games.
- if you like to feel free to clap during songs.
- if you like the talk to go into a subject in depth (and take a long time over it).

- if dancing makes you cringe.
- if you're happy to pray out loud.
- if you understand the word 'redemption'.
- if you get worried or scared when open and honest emotion is shown.
- if you love colour and brightness.
- if you hate moving out of your seat.
- if you're at church because someone else has made you come.
- if you like peace and quiet.

You might also swap cards and try the same activity again with people taking different characters.

At the end, bring everyone together and find out what insights they have gained from the activity. Ask how relevant they think it is to the congregation in your own church. Ask if any changes need to be made in the light of what they have learned.

If God had wanted us to be the same, it would have been very easy. I've been revising GCSE Science with my 15-year-old and feel that I know more than I want to know about cuttings, clones, gametes and the difference between asexual reproduction and sexual reproduction. But it's impossible to get away from the fact that human beings work best when the genes are given a good mix-up: diversity is good, even in the very building blocks of life. It is certainly messy and unpredictable and risky, but so is the creative process for artists and sculptors, poets and engineers.

Church is about life and growth, so it makes sense to look to biology for hints as to where and when growth takes place and what fosters life. For instance, the Science

GCSE mnemonic MRS GREN reminds us of the signs of life: movement, respiration, sensitivity, growth, reproduction, excretion, nutrition. These signs can be a useful way of looking at church services afresh:

- **Movement**: How much movement is there in your services?
- **Respiration**: Are your services a breath of fresh air?
- **Sensitivity**: Do all the senses get the chance to be exercised in your services?
- **Growth**: Are individuals growing in faith and understanding?
- **Reproduction**: Are people joining your church?
- **Excretion**: Do your services help people to process what's going on in their lives and leave behind anything unhelpful or burdensome?
- **Nutrition**: Are you offering a balanced and healthy range of ways to nourish all sorts of people?

Life comes from diversity. It happens on the edge of things. It is unpredictable and messy and breaks out in uncontrollable ways. Is there room for it in your church?

Church history in the UK

Let's return to the question: why, in churches, do we segregate people according to their age? One answer might be found in the history of church.

The imaginary St Sluggit's Church is typical of many UK churches in the 21st century: it has a Sunday school during the morning service. The children are 'in' for the first 20 minutes of the service, then they are prayed for and they leave for their 'session', which lasts until the 'main service' ends.

This model has its origins in the Sunday school movement of Robert Raikes, back in the 18th century. Raikes was so appalled by the degeneracy of children from impoverished households, and their lack of education, that he gathered them together on a Sunday and taught them how to read and write so that they had a hope and a future.

But hang on, let's stand back and look at this. What has it got to do with the situation in the UK today? Our children are all in compulsory education from around the age of four, being taught by lean keen professionals to read and write. The church is not called on to provide this service any longer; nor is it even qualified to do so in this day and age. So why do we send the children out of the service? Because we have always done it? Because they are happier to go than to stay? Because we want to get some heavy teaching done in 'real' church without their distracting presence? Ouch. The church has got into some bad habits over the years and, arguably, this habit of sending its children out and learning and worshipping in discrete segments of congregation is one of the worst. Why have we done it?

The Sunday schools of the 19th century were walking between general education and religious education, and gradually specialised in religious education as general education through state schools became more widespread. 'One inheritance of the twentieth century was large Sunday Schools in which children and people of all ages were taught together.'[1] One notable example of this was when George Cadbury (of chocolate fame) ran a Sunday school for boys and men. In roughly the first half of the 20th century, children were sent to Sunday school, which usually happened at a different time from the main Sunday service. Parents who only occasionally, if ever, attended church themselves would send their children to

Sunday school nonetheless: 'Sunday Schools were associated with churches but in many places had developed a separate identity. Relatively few children progressed through the Sunday School to become members of the Church.'[2] Around the middle of the century, numbers in these mega Sunday schools started to drop, perhaps because more people owned cars and had more opportunities for leisure activities at weekends. Sunday school began to be run at the same time as the Sunday service.

Aha! This is where things could have taken a whole new helpful direction, especially for those families in which both adults and children were churchgoers. But instead of trying to find a way for adults and children to worship and learn together, churches went down the road of segregation, keeping children and adults apart for Christian worship and nurture.

The Family Church Movement became increasingly popular from the 1940s through to the 1970s, especially in the nonconformist churches and in the 'Parish Communion' movement in the Church of England, which children were supposedly encouraged to attend. I suspect, however, that by this time it was impossible to reintegrate children into church services that had done without them for many years—if, indeed, children have ever played an active part in gathered church in this country. Perhaps 'family services' were one-way adaptations: in welcoming children and trying to cater for them, they didn't go the difficult extra mile and help the adults try to learn from and alongside children as well. The service pattern of St Sluggit's has become the easiest option, the option that pleases most people, young and old—worshipping in our separate ways, encouraging the children to leave for their child-centred 'activities' while the adults settle down to 'proper' church. However, is the easiest option, or the most popular option, necessarily the best way to build God's kingdom?

All-age worship in the Bible

We can compare this historical development in the UK with the biblical mandate for worshipping with all ages present. The biblical mandate has been explored in detail elsewhere by wiser writers than I am,[3] but let's look at a short outline.

It is assumed that children were present during the great Jewish celebrations and in the early Church, even if they aren't mentioned specifically. 'Households' must have held children as well as adults. Baptism must have been done for children as well as adults as households came to believe. Children must have listened to the stories about Jesus and to Paul's letters alongside the adults. We are tempted to say, 'They "behaved" in church in the old days. Why shouldn't they now? Why make any special provision for them? Let them "behave" just as adults "behave".'

Well, perhaps that's the difference: how *did* the adults behave? What if they didn't sit in rows with their heads down but bubbled with zeal, excitement and a determination to hear the latest letter from Paul, to see the latest miraculous healing? What if children were learning to be Christians in the face of daily persecution and oppression, hearing stories of people they knew standing up for their faith and changing the face of the world? What if they were praying for Stephen's widow to have enough bread to eat that week? What if they had had to hide from Roman soldiers on their way to meet with the rest of the church? There wouldn't be any incentive to 'misbehave': it would be far less interesting than what was going on around them. The faith of the adults would be a model for the faith of the children and vice versa, as new Christians joined the churches and watched what went on in them.

Perhaps, too, the children's world was far less segregated from the adults' world than it is now. They would 'belong' to a community of older people in their extended family and friends—all of whom would know them by name—and would be responsible to that community for their behaviour. If the people in the room with you are your aunts, grandfather and cousins, who know what your mum expects of you even if she's not there, you're probably going to think twice about messing about. In the suburban sprawl where I live, when graffiti is scrawled on the cricket pavilion no one has any idea who did it. In the small village I used to live in, the field of suspects was limited to two.

The Bible gives us a glorious picture of God's idea of a perfect world, an ideal to live up to in our churches: 'This is what the Lord Almighty says: "Once again men and women of ripe old age will sit in the streets of Jerusalem, each with cane in hand because of their age. The city streets will be filled with boys and girls playing there"' (Zechariah 8:4–5). It is diverse and harmonious and celebrates every age group doing what they do best under the caring, watchful eye of the others.

Ah, but that's too tidy, we groan. I've got to be part of a church that exists now, here on earth in the 21st century. We've got too many messy, unfinished component parts for it ever to operate like that biblical ideal from long ago—or that wonderfully serene icon of the Trinity you were talking about. And our whole attitude to children, as well as to older generations, has changed dramatically; our children have very different rights, responsibilities and expectations from those of first-century, let alone Old Testament, children. We have different expectations, different needs, different wants… how can we reach for the stars when every time we try, someone pokes us in the armpit?

So let's look honestly at the problems of leading a church service that tries to do things together wherever possible—an 'all-age service', as it's commonly known. Let's take the biblical principle that God created us to live and worship in diverse communities and see how that works in churches—especially, for the purposes of this book, in church services—today. To begin with, can we acknowledge right from the start that people join, belong to and leave a church for the most irrational, unpredictable and complicated reasons? We're never going to get it completely right for everybody and, even if we moved mountains and calmed stormy seas, some people would take umbrage. I expect that while everyone else was busy partying at the wedding at Cana, the ancestors of such fault-finders were moaning about the quality of the wine glasses.

Starting from scratch

Many new forms of church are springing up alongside traditional church at the moment, encouraged in some denominations by the Fresh Expressions movement. There is an opportunity today, as never before, to rethink what really matters in church and to put it into practice. We have a freedom and permission to be bold that has hardly ever been seen in the UK church before. No one will be burned at the stake for worshipping in the way that they feel called to.

One of the dangers of fresh expressions of church is that, being designed around the needs of a particular group in society, they can tend towards the homogeneous: for example, a church for moped riders, a church for young executives, a church for Goths. While this is an admirable and effective evangelistic strategy, it soon becomes clear that a church with only one sort of person in it is necessarily one-dimensional. As we've wondered before, how can we appreciate what it's like to enter the kingdom of heaven as a child if we never encounter any children? How can we look forward with confidence to a useful old age if we never meet any of the inspirational saints in their 80s who still serve God cheerfully? A colleague from the Intergenerational Forum said at a recent meeting, 'When I was a parent I needed other parents to show me how to bring up my children; now I'm older I need people to model to me how to die!' He was very serious and very joyful about it.

There is also an obvious problem with a church that is set up for and by a particular group of people: if it has any longevity at all, these people's situations will change so that they no longer 'fit' in that type of church. For example, young single people's circumstances can change dramatically in a very short period. Will they feel the need to leave their student-based fellowship so that they can belong to one that welcomes their baby, or their disabled parent who has come to stay indefinitely?

Yes, the glory of belonging to a wider church rather than just the local one is that we have the ability to move to a congregation that suits our needs and wants at a given time. However, one question that should be considered at the planning stage of any fresh expression of church is how best to reflect God by building in at least the potential to welcome all ages, even if a child / teenager / person in their 20s / elderly person seems the least likely member at the stage we are at now.

Inherited models of worship

In a traditional church, it is often considered desirable to 'lose' the children as quickly as possible in the course of a service. Fresh expressions of church provide a chance to dispense with some traditional church baggage, which might include the habit of sending children away to learn and worship separately. It is very encouraging to hear stories of churches that are making a positive effort to worship together as an all-age family, and some of these stories are included in this book. More can be found on www.freshexpressions. org.uk. Other churches, though, feel stuck with a model that they have inherited, where the children and adults expect the children to leave and are disappointed when they don't. This is much harder to deal with than a new congregation where everything is up for grabs.

Margaret Withers argues in an article on the BRF *Barnabas* website:

Some churches have decided that every service should have children and adults together. This is fine, but one has to remember to feed and challenge the regular and informed worshippers as well as including the youngest and least formed. A more common practice is to have an all-age service once a month. Nearly every church has occasional services that are geared towards families and the fringe: Christingle, Crib service, Mothering Sunday, Harvest or

Pentecost. These are usually the best-attended services of the year, so it is worth taking time to prepare them carefully so that everyone can actively take part.[4]

Margaret highlights here the fear that many have about all-age worship, namely that the more established worshippers lose out because everything is (to put it crudely) dumbed down to the lowest common denominator. This takes us back to the question: where should the real *learning* go on? Is the church service the main occasion for church members to do their learning, or should it happen elsewhere? And, if done sensitively and intelligently, couldn't an all-age service open up possibilities for worship, learning, wonder, fellowship and meeting God to happen during the rest of the week, rather than being the only occasion when we expect any of these things to take place? Again, these possibilities are so much easier to manage if expectations have not already been set by generations of learned segregation. It is also worth asking: if all-age worship means 'dumbed down' worship, is it OK for that to happen even once a month? I wouldn't want a substandard service once a month. Surely it is possible to have a regular service that challenges and feeds everybody all together?

There is definitely a valid argument that organising good all-age worship is so time-consuming that many ministers or worship leaders would find it impossible to hold such a service more than once a month, once a term or once a year. The permitted liturgies of the different denominations are provided in order to make a minister's job manageable, to give a benchmark for quality and to remove the onus of reinventing the wheel every week. In many denominations, though, the traditional liturgies have been designed on the assumption that the congregation will be an adult, literate, 'well-behaved' one. New liturgies are being provided, new flexibility is coming into play and some liturgies are indeed for all-age congregations, which are all moves to be welcomed; but the fact remains that to put on a localised, well-prepared, meaningful and imaginative service at which all sorts of different people are present is a very tough call. For many church leaders, it involves some hard thinking as they deliberately let go of leadership habits acquired over the years. A church which is asking this of its leadership team must be prepared to make allowances for the extra time and creative space that this style of worship needs. The members must also be ready to volunteer many more of their own gifts to be used in the church community, both to free the ministers' time for preparation and to enrich the gathered worship with more diverse elements than those to which the ministers personally have access. In other words, all-age worship is costly.

Who is it all for?

We come back to the fundamental question: what are we trying to do in worship? What is it all for? Is it an ordeal to get through as painlessly as possible? Is it meant to cater for the wants of the most vociferous congregation members or of those who pay the bills? For some churches, considering the demands of all-age worship will mean an honest, soul-searching process about who it's really for.

It's a shame, in some ways, that the Gospels were written by men, with the perspectives of their era so firmly in place. We've seen how children were much more integrated into adult society than they are in our culture, but I would love to know just what role women and children—the nobodies of Jesus' time—played in Jesus' ministry alongside the men, instead of having mere tantalising glimpses of his attitude to them. The twelve male disciples are clearly named, but few of the female followers of Jesus are named, and none of the children, even when they play a key role, such as providing food as the basis for a miracle. So we have a perception that the twelve disciples were the key players and everyone else had walk-on parts, but was that really the case or does it reflect the attitudes of the writers, who simply disregarded anyone without a beard? The classic case is indeed the feeding of the five thousand as described in Luke 9:14, where the number of people present was reckoned by the number of men, as if the women and children didn't even count as statistics.

Yet, when we consider crucial stories like that of Martha and Mary in Luke 10:38–42, where Mary is praised for taking a traditional man's role in listening to the rabbi, rather than the traditional woman's role of disappearing among the cooking pots, it's obvious that Jesus must have encouraged the 'nobodies' to play a huge role in his work. He was for ever moving out to the people on the fringes rather than concentrating solely on those at the religious centre. In fact, he evidently found it easier to demonstrate kingdom values outside the synagogues, the religious structures of the day. There's a very telling challenge to his disciples in Matthew's account of the feeding of the five thousand, which takes place in the wilderness of a 'solitary place'. Jesus didn't encourage the disciples to send the hungry crowds to a professional centre of nourishment but said instead, 'They do not need to go away. You give them something to eat' (14:16). People don't need to 'go away' to find Jesus' blessing; Christians don't need to drag friends into church buildings. Jesus challenges us to be spontaneous and offer others his blessing right where they are.

Jesus was criticised for spending all his time with the people everyone else despised: he longed for outsiders to be given a better place at the table. His attitude says a great deal about the church's relationship to people outside the church, but it also says much about the way we relate to each other inside the church: no one is to be excluded by reason of their birth, nationality, age or gender. Those people who appear to have the least to say must be listened to with special care. The people who behave inappropriately (shouting for Jesus' attention, climbing into undignified positions up trees, bothering him when he's tired, messing him up with oil) have something to demonstrate to the rest of us well-behaved, appropriate, conventional, good, religious people— something that goes beyond the ritual and ceremony so often associated with 'religiousness'. If we exclude and ignore our 'difficult' people, we miss learning what healing, forgiveness, new life and grace are all about. When we are trying to answer the question, 'Who is it all for?', we have to say 'Everybody,' not just 'People like us'.

Jesus didn't put children on a pedestal but he did bring one of them into the middle of the crowd of people to be presented as a model for discipleship (Matthew 18:1–4). In recent years, scholars have begun to take this model seriously rather than treating it as a pat way of saying that we need to be humble. If we don't have children in the midst of us, it makes it very difficult to realise the unsentimental, shocking nature of what Jesus offered to his disciples as a way of entering the kingdom of heaven. What does it mean to 'change and become like little children' (v. 3)? Can he really mean we have to be as vulnerable as that toddler trustingly walking off with the churchwardens? Can he mean we must learn to be as spontaneous and undignified as the four-year-olds dancing along to 'Thine be the glory'? Do we have to relearn how to insist unashamedly on getting as close to the action as we can so that we don't miss out on anything? *Can* we be as powerless, as totally dependent as the baby being held in her father's arms? If we don't have children simply being themselves in the midst of us, *we* are missing out, not only on our own developing discipleship as church members but on the whole purpose of the Church. As Mountstephen and Martin write: 'Our contention is that the church of all ages is the clearest way to embody kingdom values of welcome and reconciliation in order that the whole world might be saved.'[5]

Here's an illustration of the way the journey towards all-age worship may not be a straightforward one.

St Mary's, Greenham, Young Children's Service

St Mary's, Greenham is a medium-sized charismatic Anglican church on the edge of Newbury. Until five years ago, baptism couples were encouraged to attend the monthly 'Family Focus' all-age service, but John Clarke, the vicar, found that the couples didn't feel at ease in the service. It lasted about an hour and had quite a number of praise and worship songs, which were the regular fare of the morning congregation. It was difficult for service leaders to include preschool children effectively in an all-age service.

Inspired by reports of services elsewhere concentrating on younger children, John and his wife decided to experiment with a 25-minute service at 11.45am after the Family Focus. This was very 'hands-on', with puppets, activities and simple songs. Some of the congregation found it strange to split the family service, but the baptism couples unquestionably preferred the shorter service. Numbers have built up to about 20 on a good Sunday, and some continue coming even after moving a considerable distance away, as there is nothing similar nearby.

However, it has not been easy to integrate the parents into the main 10.30 service, and the split service can cause difficulty for families with children of different ages. Currently, John is wondering about the possibility of holding the young children's service at the same time as the main Family Focus, but more prayer and discussion are needed about this.

- How is this situation similar to your own?
- What would you advise John to do?

Conclusion

Churches have a very high calling and an impossible job in human terms. What they have to do is so unreasonable and demands so much sacrifice of things that are precious to us that it's a wonder anyone chooses to belong to a church at all! It's like being in a family: sometimes the demands made by older or younger generations are overwhelming. Wouldn't it be easier to divorce ourselves from the lot of them and hermetically seal ourselves off from any further contact with them?

As Sue Palmer writes in *Toxic Childhood*, however, 'That is what forging families is all about: adults putting themselves out so children's developmental needs are met.'[6] This challenges a church community as well as a nuclear family unit. Our 'adults' aren't necessarily our over-18s but rather our established congregation. If we, through the Holy Spirit, are as committed to each other as members of a family are through ties of dependency, then we will put the needs of the weaker members of our churches before our own needs. If we are truly committed to growing disciples and ensuring that everyone God sends to our community has the best possible chance to develop as a Christian, the people with the power need to be prepared to 'put themselves out' and make sacrifices in order to meet the needs of the more vulnerable and disempowered. The peculiar supernatural topsy-turvy reverse also applies here, because unless we can learn from the weak, the vulnerable, the ridiculous, the undignified, the challenging, the infuriating, the loving, the demanding and the trusting among us, we 'will never enter the kingdom of heaven'. We need each other.

An all-age church reflects the very nature of a diverse yet unified God. It demonstrates the integration of generations to which society as a whole can aspire, thus challenging the worldview that splits off the generations from each other in fear and hostility. It is the way that Christians have celebrated their faith for centuries. It is the best way of growing disciples.

– Chapter 2 –

How does worship happen?

As we have seen, we need to take very seriously the call to be all-age church. The repercussions for many churches are enormous, however. It would take volumes to explore every aspect of all-age church as a whole, so this book is concentrating simply on church services. We will touch on the whole-church community from which these services spring, but we're going to focus on what is often the most visible aspect of a church's attitude to its older and younger members—the regular coming-together to worship and learn about God.

Here's a silly sketch: does it ring any bells?

Children in church

> ONE and TWO deliver their lines separately, not responding to each other at all, as if in two completely different conversations.

ONE: You should have been in church today. Those children!

TWO: You should have been in church today. Those children!

ONE: Running up to the front in the middle of the service! I mean, talk about showing off!

TWO: Running up without any inhibitions to admire the beauty of the altar brasses gleaming in the candlelight.

ONE: No concentration at all! Crawling about on the floor!

TWO: Lost in wonder at God's creation—they spotted a common house spider and marvelled at it for a full ten minutes.

ONE: Lying down on the carpet! Totally inappropriate behaviour!

TWO: Relishing every opportunity to enjoy God's colourful world as the sun shone through the stained glass on to the carpet.

ONE: Fidgeting all through the opening prayer!

TWO: Shame they had no voice to shout, 'I don't understand! Let me in too!'

ONE: No discipline—they were simply chatting through all those lovely hymns.

TWO: They were enjoying fellowship with other Christians.

ONE: Laughing like that at poor Mrs Smith's unfortunate wart as she read the lesson.

TWO: Loving the humour of the camel trying to squeeze through the needle's eye.

ONE: Interrupting the sermon!

TWO: Bursting with questions, alive with curiosity, desperate to know more.

ONE: Tramping up and down the aisle.

TWO: Dancing before the Lord.

ONE: Bursting into tears so we couldn't hear the minister. Pure attention-seeking.

TWO: Throwing themselves into the story of the Last Supper with all their heart and soul.

ONE: At least they were quiet in the intercessions.

TWO: A shame that ten minutes of intercessions spoken in a monotone bored them all rigid.

ONE: After all, worship should be honouring to God.

TWO: After all, worship should be honouring to God.

Yes, I've exaggerated (I hope), but perhaps there's a grain of truth in it?

Potential problems in all-age services

'They please none of the people none of the time.'

'They turn into a performance with an "audience" that expects entertainment.'

'God's word can be trivialised, dumbed-down, reduced to a series of over-simplified children's talks.'

'In a desperate attempt to keep them happy, the children become stooges up at the front, holding up visual aids.'

'Children make a noise and nobody stops them.'

'Adults refuse to move from their seats to do anything participative.'

'They rely on masses of visuals, props and audiovisual technological input and we just haven't got the time and money.'

'It takes a great deal of skill to lead an all-age service and not everyone can do it.'

'A supposedly "all-age" service is really a children's service that adults observe from the back rows.'

For many church members, as soon as 'all-age worship', 'family service', 'intergenerational worship' or whatever term has become fashionable since this book was written is mentioned, panic or despair sets in. Yet the Church has been worshipping God for 2000 years, and, indeed, worshipping him for many of those centuries with all ages present, so surely we shouldn't be fazed by anything to do with worship? Surely, by now, we should know a bit about how to do it?

Let's take a step back and ask a larger question. What are we trying to do when we come together as a church to worship?

There are as many answers to this question as there are grains of sand on the beach or stars in the sky. Even when we've thought through some of the theological reasons, there are still all the very human, ridiculous, lovable, awe-inspiring, unpredictable, frustrating answers that have nothing to do with reason but everything to do with emotion, habit, longing and the general messiness of being human.

Here are a few. I wonder what your church would answer.

- We're trying to be heaven on earth.
- We're drawing close to God and he's drawing close to us.
- We're celebrating being the family of God.
- God's happy when we praise him together.
- Where two or three are gathered, Jesus has promised he'll be there.
- If you don't gather as a faith community, you'll soon become discouraged and disillusioned.
- We want to learn more about God.
- It's for evangelism—a time to invite people in to meet Jesus for themselves.
- We're meeting each other's needs for fellowship and friendship.
- We're meeting God through meeting other people.
- I've always been to church.
- It's the right thing to do.

- I want the children to grow up knowing what church is all about.
- We want to witness to what God is doing in the world.
- We want to receive Christ through the sacraments.

There isn't a simple answer that covers every diverse reason why we come together like this—the clever and the naïve, the boisterous and the gentle, the hungry and the satisfied, the hopeless and the hopeful, the illiterate and the literate, those in the spiritual waiting room and those on the high-speed train to the promised land.

A fun and useful activity for a group to try out is to take an image of God and see what that has to say about worship. It can shed a great deal of light on what we're doing when we come together on a Thursday evening or a Sunday morning or a Monday lunchtime.

Try taking images of God—biblical images (Shepherd, Father, King) or ideas from present-day situations (God as probation officer, webmaster, 'M' in the Secret Service…)—and using your imagination to extrapolate how worship might work for each of those images. For example:

If we think of God as a father, what might worship be like? Maybe it's like a family party, with babies, toddlers, aunts and uncles, grandparents and parents getting together to celebrate their identity as members of the same family, to show they care that they belong to each other. What memorable occasions family parties can be—the fun of renewing relationships, swapping news, enjoying each other's company… and a time when we need to grit our teeth and cope with drunken Uncle Bert, Cousin Kath's destructive toddlers and brother Fred who keeps forgetting your birthday, borrowing your lawnmower and inviting himself round for tea at inconvenient times. We'd like to snooze after lunch, but the children need to play Twister to let off some energy and Great-grandma would be hurt if we didn't spend some time listening to her reminiscences of the war.

We miss members of the family when they're not there. We're hurt, but understand if the teenagers opt out and want to chill with the Wii instead of talking to us. And how fantastic it is to spend time just being with the most loved Father of all, talking, listening, sharing problems and joys with him. But how easy it is to forget he's there when he graciously sits back and doesn't impose himself on us, wanting us to *want* to come and spend time with him.

So worship is a time of laughter and tears, of putting up with things not being just as we prefer so that everyone can get the most out of being together.

If God is a good shepherd, is the congregation like the sheep, brought safely into the fold at the end of a long day? They feel safe, with the shepherd lying across the gap in the wall to keep the wolves out. It's warm and cosy next to the other sheep, jammed in like sardines, even though the closeness can get a bit smelly and oppressive! Perhaps a sheep might prefer to be with the shepherd on its own, but that would mean the rest of the sheep would be in danger: they all have a right to the safety and warmth of the sheepfold and the intimacy with the shepherd. Or are the sheep out in the pasture, exposed to danger but safe with the shepherd, the envy of other flocks that have been left to wander around shepherdless?

So worship is a safe time, an intimate time, when God is

both close to us and completely 'other', a demonstration of complete security to a scared world.

If God is a guide on a journey, are we pilgrims or explorers who have met up on the road at an inn or pub before we set out again? It's lonely out there on the road, so it's great to meet with travellers who are heading the same way. We can tell that some are nearer the journey's end than we are, while others have only just started. We listen to the experienced so that we know which way to go when we come to the same crossroads, and we encourage those who don't feel like carrying on or have lost their bearings. Sometimes the most unlikely people have the part of the map we need for the next stage of our journey. We are refreshed and challenged by the sight of those who still have bags of energy at the end of a long day's walk. The guide is there to remind us where we're heading, to bandage the wounded, to fill up our rucksacks with food for the next stage of the journey, to show us the way.

So worship is an acceptance that we are all fellow travellers on a journey, whether we're young or old.

This approach may be helpful to those who have an imaginative learning style. It may help them to look round in church and picture the other people in the seats as fellow family members, brothers and sisters in arms, sheep of the same flock or fellow travellers.

Here are some starter ideas to use with a group:

- If God is like a father, worship is like…
- If God is like a king, worship is like…
- If God is like my best friend, worship is like…

- If God is like bread, worship is like…
- If God is like a good shepherd, worship is like…
- If God is like a guide on a journey, worship is like…
- If God is like an army captain, worship is like…
- If God is like a vine, worship is like…
- If God is like a healer, worship is like…
- If God is like a light, worship is like…
- If God is like a refiner's fire, worship is like…

Which of these images helps you most in understanding worship?

My favourite insight from using this activity on a training day is: 'If God is a light, worship is like… the window of a particular optician in Bournemouth.' The person who shared this went on with utter seriousness to describe how this optician had installed a shop window of the most expensive, beautiful glass that was kept clean and polished at all times, with a display full of brilliantly lit spectacles. No expense had been spared to make an eye-catching setting for the wares on display: those spectacles had the best possible chance to shine to the people passing by, in the hope that they would come in and try a pair for themselves. So worship can be our shop window: a very attractive, no-expense-spared, visible sign to passers-by, demonstrating the quality of the God we worship. How might we achieve this sort of worship? By careful, detailed planning, making sure that everything points towards God, and by gearing everything towards the outsider rather than those already there, allowing God's light to shine through every aspect of the worship and getting rid of anything that obscures the light.

This understanding of worship might be very different from an understanding that springs from an image of God as a healer, webmaster or furnace. No one image is complete in itself, but it might help your planning and vision if you can work out, as a team or as a church, what role corporate worship plays in your church life.

- Is worship primarily for the people of God?
- Is it primarily for God?
- Is it primarily for people outside the faith community?

Clarifying what we think we're doing gives us a foundation stone to build on. It helps a church to see what to include and what to leave for another context. If worship comes from the heart of the people of God, if it is inspired by God, and if it is done in a spirit of servanthood, these three 'primarilies' automatically and graciously flow into one another. Then, what is offered to God becomes a witness to those watching and a blessing to those taking part.

Let me give an example: one church in the north-east of England has decided that their Christian calling is to the whole of life, and that what happens during the working week, at the office, in school and in the home, is where faith really matters. They have groups during the week where the main teaching takes place, so their gathered worship on a Sunday is when they invite friends along, knowing that it will be a relaxed atmosphere in which to discuss faith issues in an engaging way, to experience a little sung worship and to observe people at prayer. The last theme that I heard they used was, 'What would Jesus say to James Bond?'—something that doesn't require you to have an exact knowledge of Deuteronomy before you can have a say! The Sunday event has a very definite role in the wider strategy of the church, but it is only one aspect of the church and doesn't try to do everything for every person. Biblical teaching happens elsewhere, and intimate worship also happens in house groups. That church knows what its Sunday service is for and can focus its activities accordingly.

Where does all-age worship fit in?

Just as it is far easier to have a purposeful Sunday service if we know that it's for a particular group of people, and that other needs are being met elsewhere, so it is far easier to plan and lead a service for a homogeneous group—people of the same age, from the same country or even the same county (in fact, let's face it, from the same street and preferably the same side of the same street). People with the same social background, or of the same gender—that would be good. People with the same reading age and the same learning preferences; people who have the same abilities and disabilities. People who are—oh yes, *please*—clones of each other and of the leader. Let's have a church of people like me! Let us make an image in our own likeness...

You may now retrieve this book from the flowerbed, where I hope you've hurled it in a fury. Then read 1 Corinthians 12. Look at the way Paul creates in lavish detail a picture of Christ's body, which is only complete because of its variety. You need each other's differences to be the whole body of Christ, he says! You cannot be his body if you all do the same job, if you're identical, and in verse 17 he holds up a fairground wonky mirror to show us how ugly and dysfunctional we would be if the balance of limbs and organs were out of kilter. 'If the whole body were an ear...'—you might like to doodle in the margin what that would look like.

The *Barnabas* ministry team has explored this passage with children through drama many times, and the lurching wobbly blob that emerges from their imaginations of what such a body would be like is both ludicrous and slightly scary. 'If the whole body were an eye...' is just deeply unpleasant. The thought of an eyeball rolling around trying to do the things a body does is somehow... wet—and so shockingly vulnerable. The body ceases to be a body and becomes an alien life form, one that is unfit for its element, one that belongs between the pages of a comic. No, God has placed the parts of the body just as he wants them to be.

On television, style gurus Trinny and Susannah encourage women to feel better about hitherto embarrassing parts of themselves. A whole programme has shown them helping women to enjoy the shape of their bottoms without resorting to plastic surgery. My daughter and I have consequently added 'Celebrate your bum!' to the stock of family catchphrases and yell it out of the car window whenever we pass my husband on his bike. It's a cry for which we need to find the equivalent in church: we need to celebrate the members of our community who, in worldly terms, are unshapely or ugly, or appear useless and embarrassing. Do we surgically remove them or do we take a leaf out of Trinny and Susannah's book and see the beauty in them, showing each other how to make the most of them and glory in them?

In 2003, hiker Aron Ralston was trapped in a canyon in eastern Utah as his arm was stuck under a huge boulder. After five days with no help on the horizon and with no water left, he took the desperate measure of cutting off his own arm with his pocketknife and staggered to find help. Self-amputation was a last resort, and, even then, an action that makes most of us feel sick at the very thought.

Paul was writing about the discrepancies emerging between the different social groups in the new Corinthian church, but he could easily have been writing to and about so many churches today. Of course, like attracts like, and we probably all know people who have sadly left a fellowship because there has been no one 'like them' there. But a church that deliberately and systematically excludes any group of people is—to pick up Paul's image and Mr Ralston's experience—like a person deliberately hacking off their own arm. Yes, it's that painful and damaging, and this applies as much to an age group as to any other group segregated by ethnicity, tradition, ability or class.

If we deliberately exclude a group of people, we are disfiguring ourselves and denying ourselves as a church the opportunity to be something that goes deeper than studying God's word, having fellowship, praying, reflecting, sharing the sacraments or all the other things we *do* when we 'worship'. What are we *being*? We might seem to be doing those things all the better for not having a particular group present, but are we actually becoming the people God wants us to be when we exclude them? Are we creating a sustainable church that will exist beyond one generation? Do we really make ourselves open to meeting God when we present in our worship an image of him that is in our image?

Perhaps he has a bigger picture in mind, a plan to bless us that goes even further and deeper than anything we can imagine—a plan that equips us and enables us to meet God in others. Maybe he has a vision of a body that celebrates its differences, its variety, that learns to delight in something different, that rejoices when surprises happen, that sees interruptions as an opportunity to learn something unexpected. Perhaps he has a plan to make us a people who can find him in the strangest of places and in the most unlikely of people. Perhaps we need to start practising in church so that we're fit to be Christians in the world.

Worship springs from community

Before we move on, another point is worth highlighting. Research has consistently indicated that if you try to set up a worship service that includes all ages without having a Christian church community that includes and celebrates all ages, you won't get very far. To build a church that does all its other activities in discrete age groups and then expects to come together painlessly on a Sunday is a tall order. Of course there need to be different activities for different groups in the life of a church. The simple demands of different lifestyles make that obvious. In our congregation there are elderly people who don't like coming out on their own after dark but want something to break up the daytime. Children, on the other hand, are busy at school during the day but have set bedtimes, so their drama group needs to finish by 8.30, while adults who are out at work don't get back home till later, and house groups cannot start before 7.30 at the earliest. A congregation like Messy Church is made up of people from all sorts of backgrounds—children rushing straight in from school, parents who have coped all day with toddlers at home and need some adult company, elderly people who don't want to be out late, people working in jobs at some distance who dash in as soon as they can get there.

We're never going to get it right for everybody every time. One thing we've realised about Messy Church is that no time of day will suit all ages and all backgrounds. Too early, and working parents can't come along; too late, and the toddlers are excluded. Many Messy Churches run at weekends to make themselves available to people who work away from home, while others can only find enough helpers to meet midweek. There are obvious practical questions that cannot be overlooked. But as soon as we start segregating groups by differentiating on the grounds of intellectual abilities, expectations of behaviour or assumptions about faith development, *any of which we are thoughtlessly linking to age*, we are on dangerous ground.

We can accept the fundamental principle that our default setting as a church is to do as much as we can with all ages present. We can do whatever we do in a way that will welcome everyone, whatever age they are, unless there is an unavoidably valid reason for segregating. Maybe it's not a huge cause for complaint if the Annual General Meeting or the course on marriage enrichment can only be held at 8pm, after the toddlers' bedtime. It is harder, though, to think of activities that children enjoy that adults would definitely not benefit from. Holiday clubs, youth camps, trips to films, meals, toddler groups—all these not only require adult assistance and leadership but can be organised in such a way that the adults learn and grow through them as well as the children. We will *want* to be together, because we will recognise that the more we struggle to get on with each other in community, the closer we grow to God.

We won't necessarily find this the most comfortable approach to worship—in fact, it can be a charter for frustration, dissatisfaction and compromise—but it is a high calling and one that a church should use to challenge the segregated secular world. Yes, there will be times when the teenagers want to blob out on beanbags or when the toddlers want to run round the hall giggling. There will be times when the adults want to sit back and listen to a meaty sermon on a tricky Bible passage, or when the Third Agers want a chance to catch up on all the news. But institutionally and systematically slicing groups off from the main body of the church can too easily become the default setting, making it hard to put in the effort to do anything with all ages present. We need to slice with surgical expertise, if at all.

Learning as we worship

We come together as a church to worship God and to learn about him. While this is not the place to analyse how worship and learning interrelate, we need to examine the assumption made by many that 'learning about God' happens primarily (or perhaps solely) through listening to a sermon. There are few children who would willingly sit and listen to a traditional sermon. Arguably, there are few of any age on the fringe of church who would willingly sit through a traditional sermon. This leaves us with a difficulty: how can biblical teaching take place if a sermon is a hard-to-handle learning medium for a large proportion of the congregation?

The issue is this: yes, we can seem to learn more effectively and comfortably in segregated groups, sending the children off to their own age-related activities while the subgroup of adults who learn best by listening can enjoy the challenges of a sermon without interruption. But is cerebral learning what church is primarily about? If church is about loving God and loving each other and transforming the world in partnership with him and with each other, can we achieve that best by splitting up or by learning to live together? If I cannot learn to cope with praying in church with a slightly smelly 80-year-old, a 15-year-old who is cleverer than I am, a toddler who wriggles or a woman who won't stop weeping, what hope do I have of loving people outside the church? Would my biblical exegesis be more effectively digested if delivered on another occasion, rather than the main gathering of the local body of Christ?

How can we best learn together how to worship God—by sending out one particular group of people who reflect his glory through their energy, imagination, lack of inhibitions and readiness to express awe and wonder, or by staying together and modelling worship and discipleship to each other? Jesus' disciples learned by listening to him, but also by being close to him and living close to each other.

If we could develop a mindset that says we learn to love God best by loving other people, young and old, and that we cannot claim to love God unless we love those around us, we would be barring the doors to prevent the children leaving for Sunday school. We would shout down anyone who suggested that the teenagers should clear off to their own room. We would put on sackcloth and ashes and beat our heads against the wall when our elderly people decided to attend only the 8am service. We would be terrified of committing the sin of idolatry if the only people in our church service were similar to us in age (let alone outlook, faith development, theology, intellect, social outlook and colour)—terrified that we would be led towards making God in our own image and worshipping what is safe and familiar and controllable, rather than risky, unpredictable and 'other'.

A Bible passage that sums this up much more succinctly than I can put it is 1 John 4:19–21:

We love because he first loved us. If anyone says, 'I love God', yet hates his brother, he is a liar. For anyone who does not love his brother, whom he has seen, cannot love God, whom he has not seen. And he has given us this command: Whoever loves God must also love his brother.

For the words 'his brother', if we substitute 'children' or 'teenagers' or 'grown-ups' or 'elderly people' or any other group of people who might belong to a church (that is, anybody at all), and if we substitute the honest 'hate' with the words 'cannot stand' or 'is afraid of' or 'never knows what to say to', we end up with a massive challenge to our churches:

If anyone says, 'I love God', yet tries to avoid children, they are a liar. For anyone who runs a mile from children, whom they have seen, cannot enjoy the presence of God whom they have not seen.

If anyone says, 'I love God', yet stays as far as possible from the elderly, they are a liar. For anyone who cannot enjoy being with elderly people, whom they have seen, cannot enjoy being with God whom they have not seen.

Imagine a church that took these words seriously! It's a bit dangerous. In my case, for instance, I've happily led Sunday school and youth groups during services for years. But as I've woken up to the thinking about all-age worship, I've felt increasingly frustrated and angry at the need for the children to leave the rest of church every Sunday. I feel complicit in a system that I no longer agree with. I want something better.

Splitting up by age

Of course, it's the easiest option to send children out (unless you're the Junior Church leader). It saves lots of imagination because the remaining adults have learned a useful passivity, which comes across as well-behaved interest and sympathy to the longest and driest of sermons or the most laborious piece of liturgy. Children haven't had as long to practise cover-up behaviour and are more prone to showing when they are bored.

It is often argued that children learn better in their own age groups, but we don't say that retired people learn better in their own age group, or that the mid-40s learn better with their own age group. Is there something intrinsically different about children? I don't think so. If we are trying to help children mature at an appropriate pace in order to gain the skills they need for adult life, we need to ask, will they learn these skills better by being removed from the faith community or by belonging to it and having the skills modelled to them by patient older members of the congregation? This isn't a rhetorical question. While I would love to come down heavily in favour of children's development benefiting most greatly from being part of a worshipping community, this requires such an effort of benevolent empathy on the part of the congregation that I'm not convinced there are many churches saintly enough to carry it through. In the real world we inhabit, perhaps there needs to be some 'children only' time in churches. But how quickly would the segregation become the norm once more?

In an article in the *Church Times* on 30 May 2008, introducing her book *Understanding Children, Understanding God*, Ronni Lamont argues the case for Sunday schools. She writes:

To equip Sunday-school teachers and children's workers properly, a church first needs to step back and engage with some fundamental questions about its ministry to children. First, why are the children separated off from the rest of the congregation?

This is usually because of two criteria. One is purely pragmatic, to do with removal of disruptive noise. The other is about the differences between adults and children. Children think differently: they have different patterns of behaviour, and have different language needs to most adults. Although adults can understand liturgy designed for children, that is not reversible, and children do not usually have the cognitive processes required to understand adult liturgies and sermons.

Leaving aside the enormous issues raised by the 'removal of disruptive noise', Ronni implies that churches which use Sunday schools believe that worship is largely about cognitive learning and 'understanding'. Yet surely there is much we need to learn as a worshipping community that has far less to do with academic learning and more to do with whole-life learning, whole-person learning. While we wouldn't expect children with shorter attention spans and limited vocabulary and life experience to sit through some lectures, concerts or plays that adults might enjoy thoroughly, here we are thinking about what is best in church worship, a different activity altogether from an academic lecture or an artistic performance.

Are we convinced that the liturgies and sermons we offer are so valuable that it is better to remove the people who can't cope with them? If not, should we be wondering instead how to adapt the liturgies and sermons to make them accessible to everybody? Is the church service the best or only time for cerebral learning to take place? Just because people have learned to 'behave' in church, it doesn't always mean that effective (cognitive) learning is actually taking place. Learning is on all sorts of levels, and good learning is not just about the mind but also about the heart. The writers of *A Good Childhood*, the challenging report from The Children's Society, say that what children need more than anything else is to receive and learn to give love: 'For this to happen, they need parents and teachers who are unselfish and from whom they learn the secret of harmonious living: putting human relationships above all else.'[7] If that is the call of teachers and parents, shouldn't the church be leading the way by example, and equipping those in nurturing positions to do their job even better?

When I was teaching in an upper school (ages 13–18), I longed for it to be a community school in the truest sense, with adults and small children learning alongside teenagers. There was so much they could have learned from each other, and French and German could have been so much more fun with a broader age range than simply students in a narrow band from 13 to 14 or 17 to 18. Within those classes, on the purely academic front, I was always conscious that there were some who had never mastered the basics of English, let alone French, and who would be happier learning with much younger children. On the other hand, some of a very young age had as firm a grasp of the concepts as GCSE or A level students. But it wasn't just French or German that they could learn: there was a whole range of life skills, like the tolerance and manners of the older generation and the unpredictable quirky humour and *joie de vivre* of teenagers, that could have benefited people of all ages. We like to segregate, however, and those teenagers never saw adults bewildered and vulnerable just like them but still dealing with it. They never saw more mature people modelling courtesy and patience. And the adults never saw teenagers grappling with a difficult concept and not giving up until they'd grasped it. They never admired the way teenagers swap moods in the blink of an eye or show the most stubborn loyalty to their friends. So, in a worst-case scenario, teenagers in a school lesson learn only from their peers—and from one isolated adult in a confrontational situation of unenforceable authority versus aggressive powerlessness. (Yes, I exaggerate.) Please tell me this latter description doesn't also apply to your church!

Conclusion

Our God is a God of exciting differences. Our worship can reflect his amazing multifaceted nature or it can be monochrome. Our worshipping community can be gloriously diverse or it can be bland. We need to treat our worship structures and patterns with discrimination and be clear about why we are worshipping at all, then frame what we do to serve that purpose. If we deliberately exclude any group of people for our own selfish purposes, we are on dangerous ground, because we are missing out on the richness of life that God wants for us all. This goes beyond the specifically 'all-age' question into the question of what it is to be an 'all-people' church and then how to worship as an 'all-people' church. All-age worship brings these issues into sharp focus, giving us the opportunity to re-evaluate what we do and are as a church and as individuals, and ponder what God might want us to become.

*

– Chapter 3 –

What matters most?

You've got it clear in your head why you're holding a service, and in particular an all-age one. Now think about how you would reply to the question, 'In a worship service, what matters most?' How do you react to the one word answer: 'Relationships'?

It is so easy to say and so hard to realise that many church services have unwittingly militated *against* the building up of relationships across the generations. Perhaps it is only when we admit we've been getting it wrong that we can consciously try to find the solution. Part of this confession is the realisation that intergenerational support may have been part and parcel of life for other faith communities but is new ground for many Christians: 'In seeking to unite differing generational strands, we're mapping new territory. It's important to bear in mind that no-one has been here before.'[8]

Institutionalised separation

The old chapel at Lincoln Prison is a sinister place. The theory, at the time it was built, was that sin could pass from one inmate to another like an infectious disease, so the 'Separate System' was adhered to in an attempt to keep the prisoners as isolated from each other as possible. The House of Lords Select Committee of 1835 recommended 'that entire Separation, except during the Hours of Labour and of

Religious Worship, and Instruction, is absolutely necessary for preventing Contamination, and for securing a proper System of Prison Discipline'.

When it was time to attend chapel, the prisoners were hooded and led into individual high-sided cubicles, rather like upended coffins, from which each person could see and hear only the preacher at the front of the chapel. It was solitary confinement in the same room as around 80 other people. Visiting the prison as a tourist and sitting in one of those cubicles, even without a leather hood obscuring my view, was a sobering experience. And yet, is it so different from the experience of many people in church services today?

The Lincoln Prison chapel might be designed to prevent anyone from relating to anyone else apart from the preacher, but do some churches unconsciously take the same attitude? Can people find themselves totally isolated in the middle of a crowd, in a relationship of complete passivity with one person who holds a position of power? Is there a fear of any sort of relationship, as that might lead to 'Contamination'? The Lincoln Prison chapel is a parable of church at its worst. Perhaps a church might echo the principle of 'Separation' in the layout of the furniture: how easy is it in your church building to see and hear other people, to observe them as models of discipleship and learn from the way they worship? Perhaps the service itself militates against 'Contamination': it may depend simply on a passive audience relating to an active director at the front. Perhaps any unsolicited participation is treated as an intrusion into the unwritten rule of silence, a breakdown in 'Discipline'. Perhaps a church service systematically excludes a certain group of people and keeps them isolated in another room...

Many of us are familiar with the sort of service where

members of the congregation sit as far away from each other as they can, while also remaining as far away from the leader as they can. If they were the body of Christ, they would be something like hands and feet on the end of very long, skinny arms and legs. Then, at the end of the service, they may make a run for the door before anyone can try—horror of horrors—to speak to them. For someone who wishes to worship in almost total isolation, this kind of service does the job very well.

A huge worship celebration can work in much the same way. It is easy to be alone in the middle of the noise and hand-waving, to remain unnoticed. Strong leadership from, say, the music group can have a tendency to focus all attention on the people at the front rather than enabling the occasion to become fully participative.

How do we best grow disciples through our corporate worship? By dividing up into segregated groups according to age? Or by modelling worship, faith, love, life to each other?

Modelling relationships

Mike Yaconelli wrote passionately in a web article about how to do successful youth ministry, claiming that the most effective way was to be church:

Not youth church, or contemporary church, or postmodern church. Just plain, boring, ordinary church. Yes, that's right. Church. The place where people who don't know each other get to know each other; where people who normally don't associate with each other, associate; where people who are different learn how to be one.

He echoes my own experience that what people need to keep them belonging is not a wacky programme of sparkling events but a 'place to grow old together'. When a group of our friends who had known each other since student days, and had seen each other move in and out of relationships and jobs, marry, have children, move house to different ends of the country and suffer illness and bereavement, gave up the commitment of an annual joint holiday, my family and I lost one of the places where we were growing old together, a place where we knew and were known. It was always difficult to be together and involved compromise from everyone, but provided something precious that was part of our make-up as a family. Church can work in the same way, providing a safe place, an identity that goes beyond what we look like or behave like nowadays. Mike Yaconelli again:

Somehow, being with a group of diverse people week after week caused a bond to be formed—a family was created, and community happened. The mystery of community became a reality. Community isn't complicated. It's just a group of people who grow old together. They stick with each other through the teenage years, marriage, children, getting old, sick, and finally dying—all the while teaching each other how to follow Christ through the rugged terrain of life.[9]

Of course there are times when we long to be insignificant and unnoticed, when we would love to pop in and out of a service without being 'pestered' by other people. There are times when we don't want anyone to notice us and we just want to be lost in the crowd. Perhaps, though, we only long for these times because we have rich (if messy) relationships to fall back on, and who says that what we want is what's best or right for us anyway? Sometimes we might sneak off to a quiet Taizé-style evening service or a massive guitar-led celebration where no one knows us, in order to concentrate on God without the distractions of all the various jobs we have to do in our own church community. That is quite different from deliberately avoiding human contact on a permanent basis in case others should make demands on us. If we are genuinely trying to follow Jesus, anything that tempts us to opt out of relationships on a long-term basis is risky, as walking in his footsteps is all about relationships in their diversity, dirt, danger, disappointment and glory.

But, you may be saying, surely a church service is all about God, isn't it? It's not a time for building up relationships with each other. That can happen elsewhere. Surely church services are about focusing entirely on God.

Jesus and relationships

Yes, church services *should* reflect the identity of God, especially God in Christ, but they should also reflect the identity of his people in that place at that point in history.

If a church service reflects God, it should reflect him in the wholeness of his relationships. The Rublev icon shows us Jesus outside time, living together with the other persons of the Trinity. John writes, 'In the beginning was the Word, and the Word was with God, and the Word was God' (John 1:1). Right from the beginning, Jesus was in a conversation, in a story, in a chat; and he was the conversation, the story, the chat. From the beginning, Jesus has been in a dynamic, news-swapping, storytelling, close and intimate relationship. No wonder he's good at it.

Jesus could have come to earth in any form, with any

background. What background did God choose to place him into? First a family, then a village, then a group of close friends and supporters. He could have chosen to place his Son into the world fully grown and independent, or (like Romulus and Remus) into the care of animals, or isolated from ordinary human contact in a palace. Jesus could have chosen to become a great hermit, dispensing wisdom from a distance and living in a desert. He could have decided to work alone and remain free from all the problems that other people bring with them. He could have died for us without once being in touch with us. Instead, all his life, from his very conception, Jesus was in intimate contact with other human beings. Luke reports that, even as a twelve-year-old, he didn't run away from his parents to spend time wandering the streets of Jerusalem alone, but was driven to be with the best teachers of the day, listening and talking (Luke 2:41–52). He did go off and have time on his own with his Father, of course, most notably in the wilderness at the very start of his work (Luke 4:1–2), as well as spending early mornings and late nights praying on hilltops (Mark 1:35; 6:46), but his main work was breaking down barriers between people and healing relationships between them and between them and God—to bring all things in heaven and on earth together under one head, even Christ' (Ephesians 1:10).

If a church service also reflects the identity of God's people, there is a strong case for an emphasis on relationships for this reason as well. A church can be seen as an example of the fullest, richest, most wholesome life that human beings can live together.

I was surprised by a friend's sharp intake of breath as we walked along the Chesterfield canal towpath. 'Look at this!' she hissed. 'Can you believe it? How incongruous is that?' I looked at the narrowboat at which she was pointing surreptitiously (in case its owners were on board). Its name was *Shalom* and it displayed a sticker of the Christian Narrowboat Owners' Association with the Christian fish symbol. She was amazed to see this wonderful word of wholeness and healing linked with the Christian faith rather than the Jewish faith. It had never occurred to her that '*shalom*' at its best was what Jesus was all about, bringing wholeness and healing to everyone he met and ultimately to the world, on a level we can't begin to understand. In Jesus we are offered a fullness of life and relationships made possible by one who never needed a 'problem page'.

Relationships reflecting Jesus

I've been learning about the Beatitudes (Matthew 5:1–12) with my Junior Church group, who currently range from three to eleven years old. As a description of how we should get on with living our lives, they are superb. It's been very interesting to discover what I, as an adult, take for granted. For instance, we read together, 'Blessed are the pure in heart, because they will see God.' There was a blank look.

'What's pure?'

'Um, well, I suppose it's if you aren't damaged in any way, if you're not rotten inside.' (I was floundering a bit here.)

'You mean, like a banana when it hasn't got any brown bits?'

'*Exactly* like a banana when it's all perfect and yellow; that's exactly right!'

The Beatitudes—a sort of manifesto for Jesus' work—set out a life lived in healthy relationship. They describe people who don't think too much of themselves, people who are ready to admit their need as well as to give, people who work their socks off to get a good deal for others, people who can forgive, who can make peace, who can stand up for what's right, people who are right on the inside, like those beautiful yellow bananas.

This leaves us with the inescapable truth that one of our default settings as Christians has to be to copy Jesus and to follow his teaching and example. Whatever we're doing, we need to break down barriers and heal relationships, building people up so that they can live life to its full, whatever that means for them in their very different contexts. So relationships are at the heart of all we do as Christians, including our corporate worship. A service is (or should be) a time to break down barriers and heal hurts that divide people from each other and from God, and to give space for God to build and rebuild people's relationships with him and with each other. Sorted! If only it was as easy to put into practice.

Dr Keith White, a lecturer and director of a residential community caring for children, writes about an ideal church's job:

Churches will not routinely choose to split the family by age, so that its members find themselves separated for much of the worship and other activities. Rather, churches will want to model a variety of relationships in society, which might include family, clubs, teams, associations, communities of scholars, assemblies, parliaments and informal friendships.[10]

This takes the job of relationship-building beyond the inward-looking 'it's good for us' attitude and into the sphere of modelling relationships to the communities in which churches operate. It becomes a mission focus in itself. It means that churches can set a trend for inclusivity and pioneer the way for other organisations in society to follow. It is a way of being salt and light to the world.

How do we 'do relationships'?

It's very interesting to try to define what makes good relationships. A debate on Radio 4 on the subject of 'What makes us British?' was fascinating because of the answer given by a British Pakistani person, whose parents had been attracted to the UK by what they perceived as the 'Britishness' of the culture. By that, they didn't mean great expressions of our nationhood, like the lyricism of the National Anthem or our expertise at putting on a coronation. No, they meant things like the habit of queuing and holding doors open for people and not dropping litter in the street. Similarly, the whole question of 'How can we get our relationships right?' seems a massive one but boils down to very small acts and attitudes that represent something much deeper. It's not about putting your entire congregation through week-long personality enhancement courses so that they can be at one with each other and with themselves. It starts with actions that, in themselves, seem insignificant but build up with other similar acts to form a habit. As the saying goes, 'Sow an act and you reap a habit. Sow a habit and you reap a character. Sow a character and you reap a destiny.' Sow a mustard seed and you reap a shelter, a refuge and a safe space of growth. Sow a wheat seed and you reap a hundred times more than was sown. Sow a little yeast in the dough and the whole lump rises. That seems to be the pattern of the kingdom.

I once visited a church where no one knew me, and, as it

happened, I didn't really want to get stuck into conversation about who I was. I was greeted in a friendly way by the people at the door and, when I sat down, the person in front of me swivelled round, beamed at me and swivelled back. They were small actions but enough to make me feel welcome, small things that mattered. I wonder what might be important in building up relationships between people in your congregation. How do you show how much you care? Is it in the way every person, young and old, is greeted by name as they come in or as they come to the Lord's table? Is it the way someone has taken the trouble to check that there's enough loo paper or that there's somewhere to change nappies? Is it in remembering to ask about a difficult work situation, mentioned last week? Is it being aware of which exams students are going through at the moment? Is it the imagination shown by having a box of tissues and a dish of cough sweets at the back of church? Is it the smile that goes with the cup of coffee or the word of thanks for a job done? These are tiny issues in themselves but are all significant in that they demonstrate care for other people, which in turn provides a sense of belonging, of mattering, of identity. No one is too young or too old, too important or too unimportant to demonstrate this sort of care. The nurture of good relationships is part of the identity of a church and should be reflected in every part of its life, including its services.

Substance, not style

Good relationships have nothing to do with the style of service in which we are taking part—on one level, at least. Formal or informal, BCP Matins or a spontaneous sing through worship songs as the Spirit leads, Taizé chants or alternative worship stations—all of these can be carried out with an awareness of the importance of good relationships or with a total disregard for it. For this reason, appropriate all-age worship has much less to do with the outward form of the service than with the attitude of the people taking part. The form of a service on its own is not going to attract people of all ages. We can't say arbitrarily that because someone is a child, they must like singing so-called 'children's songs', or that because someone is a teenager, they must despise all ritual. Some children and adults need an expression of mystery, religious language and formality; some need church to be an extension of their home. Neither is intrinsically right or wrong. Thinking about and planning good all-age worship needs to go deeper than the outward forms of worship; it needs to go right to the very heart of our relationships with God and with each other.

I don't remember Jesus criticising the Pharisees for the form of their worship: it was their hypocrisy and concern for empty rituals, where they had lost sight of the reason for doing certain actions, that Jesus attacked. It's a sobering thought that we can lay on the most exquisite, moving, well-thought-out act of worship in the world—either with brilliant PowerPoint slides, slick music and a choice of 16 types of coffee, or with candles, incense and choirboys by the score—but if we have no love, if our relationships are up the spout, we really are just like foil dishes crashing together or like cymbals played by a drummer on crack cocaine. It's all noise—on the surface, maybe a lovely noise—but nothing more.

Here's an old story about this very danger. It is taken from the *Children's Kairos* (a diocesan strategy for growth) material written for the Diocese of Portsmouth. It's a lovely traditional story and I have no idea where it comes from—so apologies to the original author.

The singing monks

The monks loved to serve God in lots of different ways. They prayed and gave weary travellers a bed for the night. They looked after sick people and sang praises to God in their services. But the years passed and the monks grew old. Although their hearts were truer to God than ever, their voices grew cracked and hoarse. Their once-beautiful singing sounded like a farmyard of animals honking and squawking and wheezing. The Abbot was very troubled. 'This singing sounds terrible!' he said to the brothers. 'Brother Andrew sounds like a strangled turkey! Brother Francis sounds like a dying pig! Brother Mark sounds like a squashed frog! How can this awful noise be pleasing to God?' The monks agreed to pray about it.

That night a stranger arrived at the monastery door. He was a traveller who had lost his way and needed a bed for the night. The monks welcomed him in and gave him hot soup and fresh bread. 'Where are you going?' they asked him. 'To the National Opera House,' the young man replied proudly. 'I am an opera singer and I have a big part to sing in the gala next week.'

'A singer?' said the Abbot. 'What a godsend! Could you possibly sing instead of us in the service tonight? Your voice would do far greater honour to God than the sounds we make.'

The opera singer was delighted to show off in front of the

old men. 'I'll show them how to sing!' he thought.

That night, the chapel was filled with his glorious voice, echoing through the chapel like the voice of an angel. The monks were so thrilled that they forgot to pray. They thanked the young man and went to bed, marvelling at what they had heard.

That night, the Abbot had a dream. In his dream, God spoke to him and said, 'What was the matter with my dear servants? Why did no one sing for me in the chapel tonight?'

'Lord,' said the Abbot. 'At last we could give you real praise tonight. Didn't you hear the wonderful singing?'

'I heard nothing from the chapel tonight,' said God sadly. 'Usually it is your love for me that I hear, not the quality of your voices. But that young man only loved himself, so I could hear nothing at all.'

The Abbot woke up and told the other monks his dream. They were all deeply ashamed that they had forgotten to pray to God the night before. They asked God's forgiveness and then they were filled with such joy that they thought their hearts would burst. God loved them! He had missed them when they didn't sing! They rushed to the chapel and lifted up their voices in praise once more. In heaven God smiled. He didn't hear the wheezing, gasping and croaking. It was their love that he heard once again.

Safe space

A good touchstone that we should put in place at this point in our thoughts is the importance of creating a safe space within worship. Martyn Payne writes on the BRF *Barnabas* website about the insights that work with children can bring to our thinking about the church. The final point he raises is to do with the heart of worship.

And finally—as if all this wasn't subversive enough—our work with children also calls us to question what is really important in helping people to come close to God. Although we as leaders can spend much time (perhaps too much time!) creating exciting programmes, looking for new styles of storytelling, inventing fun games and clever prayer activities and learning lively songs, what all children's leaders very soon realise is that what really matters is developing a relationship with each of the children in our care. Jesus showed us how to do it, as he related individually to the children he came across in his ministry, whether it was to heal, to bless or to welcome them. We know that, whatever we do within our time together, the most important thing is to create a safe place where each person is known by name. This is fundamental to everything. It is only in this context that we have time and space in which our spirits can seek and respond to God's Spirit; it is in this place that faith can be nurtured as we share together our Christian story and play with that story in creative ways. This way of being together becomes the model for encountering God in our midst, as we grow in trust and meet God in each other as well as in other transcendent and mysterious ways. No wonder children's leaders often report that their children much prefer the group time than being together in the 'Family Service'. And what does that have to say to us as a church? How can the wider church community become a similar safe place to encounter God like this, where each person can teach the other to experience and come close to the living God?[11]

We're all aware that there are oodles of service orders, liturgies, handy hints and 'how to' guides for leading all-age worship, but these ideas about relationships are at the heart of it all.

They will make the difference between a genuine, caring all-age Christian community and church, and one that pays lip service to the outer forms but misses the true meaning of church—a concern for wholeness of relationship with God, with each other and with those who still haven't recognised God's love.

'Safe space', as Martyn mentions above, is a useful concept to work with when we think about how best to worship corporately in our local context. It's only when we feel safe that we can take risks, voicing our doubts and fears as well as our certainties. It's only when we trust that we can take hold of gifts like confession and absolution; that we can bring our creativity into dynamic play with God's word without fear of being slapped down. Frances Wolf, a music therapist who worked with the visually impaired, once said in conversation, 'Hate isn't the opposite of love; fear is the opposite of love. Perfect love casts out fear.' If, in our worship, we can build a space where people feel free of fear, safe to encounter each other and to meet some part of God both through each other and through his word, through the mystery of sacraments and whatever strange ways God chooses to use, we're getting something right.

Perhaps that's partly why Jesus got so uncharacteristically worked up against the Pharisees: they had managed to turn actions which were supposed to be helpful, which were meant to create a community of justice and peace, into a restrictive set of rules. Following God, for them, was like one of those party games involving an electric wire over which you have to guide a wire loop: if you wobble just once, a buzzer goes off and you've lost the game. When religion becomes no more than a list of dos and don'ts, rules and regulations, taboos and no-go areas, it becomes something to fear and to get wrong rather than something to bring life and choice. It also creates a select few who know the rules and can correct others who are less knowledgeable. It becomes a matter of doing the right things to get right with God, rather than putting your hand in God's and seeing where he takes you. No wonder many people don't want any part of it! If you're made to feel worried about when to sit, stand and kneel, or if there's a bewildering array of apparently meaningful but incomprehensible gestures to try to copy, a church service will be an exhausting and embarrassing ordeal. That's especially true if you find yourself sitting at the front, an experience we once had at a funeral service, which gave me chronic neck strain from twisting round too often to keep an eye on what everyone else was doing.

What makes up 'safe space'?

If we use the touchstone question 'Does this help create a safe space?' to assess everything we do in all-age worship, we can get a good idea of what is helpful and what isn't.

Here are some typical component parts of a service to which we might apply this touchstone: 'Are we creating a safe space?'

- As people come in… do we welcome them by name or find out their name? Do we treat everyone with equal respect, however old or young they are? Do we make our expectations or lack of expectations clear to them?
- As the service starts… do we make it clear why we're here, how long we're going to be here, or how much noise we're allowed to make? Do we explain who the speaker is?

- When we confess what we've done wrong… do we allow time and space for reflection? Do we demonstrate that God is desperate to forgive anything we've done wrong? Do we encourage honesty—or hypocrisy?
- If we sing or use music… does the volume encourage us to worship? Are there times to listen as well as to sing? How would others react if we used the music differently—clapped, danced, conducted using a cuddly elephant, knelt, remained silent?
- When we pray… how do we make sure people have the chance to bring their prayers to God? How do we help them know God hears every prayer?
- In the language we use… can most people understand most of the words? When we use 'difficult' words or phrases, is there a good reason for using them?
- When we open the Bible together… how do we help people to feel safe if they can't read? How do we encourage questions? How do we expect to grow?
- In the transitions between the different service elements… do we carry people through or do we drop them down the gaps?
- When we get ready for Communion… how do we combine mystery and accessibility?
- At the end of the service… is there a discordant jarring between the service and the rest of life? Is there a dead space when no one knows what they should be doing?
- In the building we use… is it warm? Is it accessible? Is there enough light to see? Does it smell damp and decayed or fresh and clean? Are there unnecessary sharp edges or dangers? Is it clean? How is colour used?

Of course, added to all this we need a healthy dollop of discernment: for every ten people who love being welcomed by name there will be someone who finds it intrusive. For all those who love to walk into a bright clean church, there will be someone who yearns for darkness and mystery, the scent of ancient hymn books and bat droppings. People are gorgeously complicated, which is why we need healthy relationships, built up through the rest of the church's life in apparently insignificant acts and words, so that there is grace running through all our well-meant mistakes and blunders.

Building relational worship

What can a church put into practice as it seeks to improve its relationships?

- First, look for the networkers—those who thrive on being with others, who always know when the next party's happening. Affirm these people's gift and help them to see it as God-given and hallowed within the life of the church. Encourage them to open their eyes to see ways to use it to build up webs of friendship that remain open to newcomers.
- Second, in everything that the church does—meetings, services, house groups, talks, flower festivals, outings— build in as part of its identity a time for listening to people, just as a church builds in time to listen to God.

Here are two examples of all-age worship from an urban and a rural setting. What do these groups do to help build up good relationships? What ideas do they inspire in terms of the community in which you worship?

Ruth Wills, a Scripture Union evangelist in the north-west of England, writes about 'Sanctus2nds'.

It takes place on the second Sunday of every month in Manchester. The layout is in café style, with small tables and chairs as well as adult-sized. The service opens with a child-friendly liturgy and the lighting of candles, followed by a story, film clip, slideshow or similar, to set the scene.

The next part of the service provides the opportunity for people of all ages to spend up to half an hour exploring three 'spaces': creative space, café space (with an activity such as a wordsearch or quiz) and prayer space. The activities encourage community, discussion and collaborative partici-pation in the creative space, personal reflection in the prayer space, and refreshment of the body in the café space. There is also an under-5s play space. Because of the creative and open-ended nature of the activities, there is scope for God to speak and for each person to make a response to him in their own way.

As an example, a painting activity that took place on Remembrance Sunday spoke of how a church should be: each member contributed to a 'group' painting on to a canvas which used red and white paint to depict feelings and responses to the horrors and bravery displayed in war. Everyone had a part to play in the painting, and even a two-year-old with his paintbrush had a really good paint. Everyone took part and made their mark. The level of 'skill' involved was not important. It was the involvement that mattered and the painting represented something from each person—young to old. It was also an organic exercise, which kept on changing and growing as other people added to it. It was not a static piece, painting neither to order nor to instruction. All were able to express creativity in their own way.

The service concludes with an act of Holy Communion for all around small tables. The closing liturgy reflects back on the service and sends all out into the next week with the removal of the candles as a symbol that Christ goes with us.

The service is a space for reflection as well as the opportunity to work and talk together in an inclusive and culturally relevant community. Although numbers at this service have stayed the same for a couple of years, a 'core' group of participants have remained, the sense of family and community is evident and new people are always made to feel welcome. Therefore tea and toast are made and served by the children before everyone goes home.[12]

Here is a rural example adapted with permission from the Fresh Expressions website.

The parish of Hope has a population of about 6000, living in five villages near the English border. After a confusing pattern of service times, a form of all-age worship was introduced at a different time from previous services. The advantage of this timing was that no one would attend expecting anything even vaguely liturgical. The worship is usually led by members of the Sunday Club team.

We meet in the new area of flexible seating and sit in a circle. This helps parents of small children limit their movements. It also encourages a new aspect of worship: namely, we talk to each other at various points in the service.

The main challenge is for the worship to be genuinely

all-age. We begin with a question for discussion in twos and threes which anyone can answer. For example, when the theme was 'forgiveness', taken from the Gospel for the day, the question was, 'What is the most difficult thing you've had to do this week?'

Answers included 'sums' and 'getting down to DIY' but also 'forgiving someone'. After that, everyone felt that they owned the subject. When we were celebrating Epiphany the answer was non-verbal—those present were asked to choose one item out of a selection of objects to give to a newborn infant.

We often discuss another issue in small groups later in the worship and then share our conclusions together. Small children are given an opportunity to draw, colour or model something to do with the subject.

We are as likely to listen to a CD of modern Christian music as to sing.

Most people take part in the intercessions. Mainly they choose from a selection of one-line prayers printed on slips of paper in advance, which express the theme.

The refreshments are all part of the worship. Squash and biscuits are served towards the end of our time together rather than afterwards. In this, as in other aspects, we have drawn inspiration from Godly Play and from cell church.

It's interesting that when numbers exceed the mid-20s and a second row of chairs has to be added, the atmosphere is not quite the same. Perhaps one of the values of this sort of all-age worship is its intimacy.[13]

Conclusion

If we want to belong to a church that reflects God, reflects Jesus, develops his ministry to everyone and is a foreshadowing of heaven with 'a great multitude… from every nation, tribe, people and language, standing before the throne and in front of the Lamb' (Revelation 7:9), then we have to take seriously the question of what matters most in our church services. Are we prepared to reconsider what we do from the point of view of healing relationships on a local and cosmic level? Do we really want to create safe spaces for people of all kinds to come close to God or do we want to maintain a safe space for ourselves—even if that safe space has grown into an impenetrable carapace (made of taste, fixed expectations, self-satisfaction, fear or other church-induced limitations) that prevents us from coming close to God or others from coming close to us? In the following chapter we will think about practical ways in which we might start to make changes.

*

– Chapter 4 –

Rules of thumb for all-age services

How can we help different people worship together in a church service? What activities are accessible to most of the people most of the time and don't exclude specific groups? How might we include these activities in a traditional service or in a service for people who don't yet come to church?

Here is one list of general guidelines. I'll include another in a later chapter to demonstrate that these aren't golden rules or set in stone. Rather, these are general principles to try out, bear in mind, adapt and develop.

- Keep it simple
- Use the senses and emotions
- Use story
- Include participation
- Use invitation
- Be real

Keep it simple

If you've got a roomful of people of different ages, backgrounds, stages of life and so on—not to mention people who have come from a variety of activities just before church—it makes sense to focus on one theme and to make everything echo that theme, develop it and amplify it. This will be more effective than galloping madly in all directions, drawing in a Gospel reading about fish, an Old Testament psalm about the wrath of God, a set prayer about evangelism and inter-cessions for healing. Repetition with variation is a good idea during the service, partly because it will help ideas to sink in slowly through reinforcement. The old advice on writing an essay works in a similar way: say what you're going to say, say it, and say what you've said. If you're going on a journey as a church during a service, you want to go on it together, visit the same places and have something in common to discuss and reflect on. It takes time to gather people from their very different preoccupations in order to embark on that journey.

Just as you plan a holiday to take into account whatever different members of the family want to do, so you'll plan a service to take into account aspects of a theme that different groups of people might appreciate and through which they might draw closer to God. Imagine a three-generation family —grandparents, parents and children—visiting a city. The children have never been there; the grandparents have been there often and have a wealth of memories and experiences of different parts of the city. Now, though, they are visiting the old familiar places with the questions and observations of a new generation, so they see those places with a fresh eye. The children, who might otherwise never think of visiting particular parts of the city, step into them with the reassurance of their grandparents' presence. The parents, meanwhile, may enjoy simply observing the relationship being built between the other two generations—and having some time out to see a familiar place with adult eyes. (Of course, the grandparents might be shocked that the children don't appreciate the same aspects of the city as they do, and the children might be frustrated that their grandparents don't whizz round it at the same pace as them, while the parents might have sloped off somewhere for a quiet drink while they have the chance. Families are messy like that, but going somewhere together is all part of being a family.)

How might this apply to a church service? A service on 'Jesus the good shepherd' where only adults are present might take it for granted that everyone knows what a shepherd is and might gloss over the idea, keeping it as something tidy, clean and hygienic instead of exploring the realities of a shepherd's life. There would be, arguably, no need to show a picture of a sheep, to bring a sheep into church, to talk to a modern-day shepherd or show a film clip of *One Man and His Dog*. It might be tempting to go straight into the spiritual imagery. However, a service with children present might involve explaining exactly what a shepherd is and does. In exploring the reality behind the image and the nitty-gritty of a shepherd's tasks, a shepherd's position in first-century society, and a shepherd's concern for the animals in her or his care, everyone can benefit from a fresh and real understanding of what Jesus is talking about in John 10.

By visiting the old and familiar in the presence of those who have never been there before—or, indeed, in the presence of those to whom this is a wonderful yet familiar space— everyone can enjoy the benefits of a different viewpoint. Remember, though, that it won't ever be as tidy and squeaky-clean as that, any more than a family holiday is an unmitigated joy for each person from start to end.

Keep things simple: try to focus on one theme for the whole service and make everything reflect that theme in some way so that everyone can travel together. If the theme is the good shepherd, let there be shepherds in the welcome, sheep in the songs, wolves in the talk, green pastures in the prayers, and feasts in the dismissal.

Avoid unnecessary, superfluous or inconsequential gimmicks. We've all been to (and, I admit it, led) services with a wacky gimmick of some sort that seems such a good idea at the time. But afterwards there's that sneaking feeling that people will remember the gimmick and forget why it was used. There was an exploding cockatoo. Because...? There was a blow-up dinosaur behind the second row of chairs. Because...? The music group abseiled in from the gallery. Because...? A gimmick is great as a hook to hang a theme or a point on, but not as a cheap thrill for the purposes of entertainment. Of course, it's all very subjective and one person's gimmick is another person's visual aid.

It's worth asking at each stage of the service planning: do we *need* to change what we normally do in this part of the service? Change for the sake of change is time-consuming and unnecessary. If it can be kept simple, why not keep it simple? Might it help people feel at home in other services if there is a more-or-less familiar pattern to the worship throughout the month? If the best way of opening up this particular part of God's word is by simply reading the passage from the lectern Bible, why add a bubble machine and a troupe of jugglers? (There again, if the passage is enhanced by bubbles and jugglers, why not? Though it's hard to think which passage that would be...) A default setting for a service can save everyone a lot of time and tension: there's no intrinsic need to be different every time. Indeed, human beings thrive on ritual and repetition as much as on variety and novelty.

Simplicity is also a useful touchstone in terms of the language used. There are some religious words for which it's hard to think of a replacement—for example, 'grace', 'baptism' or 'love'. But other religious words are better explained or left out in favour of a simpler everyday equivalent—such as repentance ('turn our backs on things that make God sad'); resurrection ('Jesus/Lazarus coming back to life'); salvation ('God's rescue plan'). I was accosted by a member of a church the other day who demanded, 'Does your vicar have a chasuble?' To her, a chasuble is everyday workwear; to me it sounded peculiarly incongruous, like asking if the vicar has an embarrassing disease. Every group of human beings has a tendency to develop its own jargon, its inner-sanctum-speak: it's worth consciously deciding which ecclesiastical words are helpful and which are obfuscatory. Again, it can be very refreshing to try to express what 'sin' or 'blessing' or 'kingdom' or 'absolution' means, rather than carelessly using the religious word as a shorthand for something we feel people ought to know already.

Of course, some people enjoy the more traditional ecclesiastical language. It's colourful and can encompass a wider meaning than a wishy-washy explanation or definition might. 'Redemption' is perhaps one such term, which has a wonderfully rich etymology that might be lost in a simplistic definition. So, if we use these technical terms, let's use them deliberately and with care, to clarify rather than muddle, to empower rather than disempower. Ask primary school teachers how they explain new words to a class when they come across them in a book. How might a secondary school teacher explain a technical term? Can you learn from them? When did anyone last explain to your church what 'Amen' means?

Use the senses and emotions

I wonder which part of ourselves we subconsciously leave outside the church door.

Perhaps, for some, they leave their critical faculties: they don't expect to be stimulated intellectually once they get inside. Thinking or reflecting on the theme of the service is not expected of them. Coming away with new ideas or mental challenges is simply not going to happen. Mental challenge comes from other spheres of life: it's hardly something one expects to be faced with in church.

For others, maybe their emotions are left outside. They expect the whole experience of church to be on a purely impersonal, objective, ritual level that doesn't touch them in any way.

Some may leave their senses out in the cold. All that has ever been required of them in church has been 'words'— sung, listened to or spoken. The idea of using touch, smell and taste, sight and listening in anything other than an incidental 'My word, it's cold in here!' or 'Goodness, we must get the drains unblocked!' sort of way is unthinkable.

Maybe some people wouldn't lose much if they left their body outside and came in, if it were possible, with just a bottom (for the sitting bits) with no arms or legs, hands or mouths, with which to wave, hold people up before God, walk, run, clap, dance, kneel or smile.

Or perhaps some people even (heaven help us!) abandon their spirituality. From experience they know that church is not going to help them with the questions they are asking— the deep doubts and joys, their yearning for the unattainable, their hunger for meaning, their awareness of otherness and mystery. Awe and wonder come to them in other spheres of life—through the arts, perhaps, or intellectual debate, nature or meditation—but not through church worship.

This has been said so many times about all-age worship that it is a cliché, but it's still worth repeating because it is so important and because it still doesn't happen enough in our churches: we need to encourage worship with our whole selves. God made us to be fully functioning human beings, with a wide range of ways of understanding the world, each other and him. The mind is important, of course, but so are the five senses, the imagination, the emotions and the body. In her novel *Miss Garnet's Angel*,[14] Salley Vickers describes the eponymous heroine on a spiritual journey from dry, cold intellectualism to emotional awakening through the extravagant colour and beauty of Venice—found, incidentally, among other places and people, in a church. The appeal to her senses cuts through all the barriers she has put up against anything that touches her at her core. We need a range of experiences within our church services to help us become whole and balanced disciples. Jesus was a whole person as no one before or since has been whole. He not only relished a keen intellectual debate from an early age, but also loved food, touched people, watched flowers and animals, spat, wept, expressed amazement, delighted in God and people, shouted, dripped with perfume and hurled furniture around.

The senses are also an accessible, inclusive way for all ages to come close to God and to each other. In fact, they are one of the more obvious areas in which children can lead the way and remind adults what it is to be fully alive, fully human. A baby learns not by perusing learned tomes but by stuffing things in her mouth to taste them. A toddler tries to touch everything in sight. An eight-year-old runs from one thing to another, cartwheeling, crawling, jumping, shoving and delighting in the way his body bursts with energy.

You don't need to have a theology degree to taste wine or to smell fresh bread. A five-year-old can enjoy singing or listening to music as much as a 50-year-old. Watch your children in church: one of our toddlers was far too young to be able to sing the hymn in a recent service, but was actively joining in by keeping time with a stuffed toy and listening to and watching her grandmother in whose embrace she was standing. Like someone learning a foreign language by listening, that child was fully engaged at one level and simultaneously taking the first steps towards corporate worship at another.

Are children too young to imagine how it feels to be afraid or joyful or amazed? Perhaps the problem is more that older generations have come to see anything experiential as childish and beneath them. Certainly that's one of the challenges we face in Messy Church during the craft time. The adults are happy to encourage and help the children to make and draw, but you can see the panic cross their faces when they are invited to make something themselves. We very soon learn, as adults, to shut down our creativity and avoid situations of risk. Unless we feel that we are 'good at art' or 'good at music', we don't feel qualified to have a go and we don't want to risk failing. At a Messy Fiesta training day, one woman, a minister in her later years, held up a pipe-cleaner pencil top she had created, her face positively glowing with pride, and said, 'This is the first thing I've ever made.' Why has she never delighted in making things before, when it obviously gave her so much pleasure and brought her spirituality to life?

When we based an all-age service on a reflective reading of Colossians 1, with visuals, we asked everyone to get into groups to create a picture as their response to different verses from the reading. It was the children who dared put pen to paper first of all. The adults in our group were happy to provide ideas and suggestions but didn't want to risk 'not being able to draw'.

In worship that attempts to appeal to all ages and stages of life, we may have to consider gently retraining our churches to appreciate the tools God has given us for coming close to him. We need a whole-church approach that celebrates creativity all week round, all year round, inviting people to experience God in other contexts through the senses and emotions, with children and adults being encouraged to learn from each other. We need adults, teenagers and children who will model worship that takes risks. Think, for example, of the different stories that might come from a group of different-aged people who are deliberately tasting bread together—the memories it might evoke, the stories some could tell, the freshness of perception others might express. By accepting and celebrating our varied responses to the different stimuli that are accessible to all, we can grow in our understanding of and relationship with each other as well as with God.

'Proper' church doesn't mean sitting rigidly in a seat, denying ourselves anything that's a delight, other than a titter at the minister's joke. It's about being the whole person we were made to be within the whole body that Christ has given us. It's part of the 'building on the rock' that Jesus talks about in Matthew 7:24–27: developing a discipleship that outlasts the storms of life because it goes deeper than our intellectual understanding or our feelings at any given moment.

How about trying this prayer idea by Martyn Payne in your church? With something to focus on, people of all ages may well find it a more helpful way of praying than simply 'hands together, eyes closed'.

Praying with colour

The idea is to focus on those who are trapped within one 'colour' for some reason. Introduce a cube with different-coloured faces. As you turn it around slowly, pause at each colour to let it remind the church of a group of people to think and pray about quietly. For example:

- Yellow: think about those who may be ill or in pain today.
- Red: think of those who may be angry for some reason today.
- Green: think of those who are jealous and envious of others today and therefore restless inside.
- Blue: think of those who, for different reasons, are sad today.
- White: think of those who are 'white with fear' today, afraid of something they can't easily share.
- Brown: think of those who are fed up and bored today and might need cheering up.

Pause and invite people to think about how they might help those who are feeling trapped. Pray that God will open their eyes to the full spectrum of beautiful colours in the world.

Drawing on art

Again on the visual front, who could fail to feel enriched by the display of a painting to explore alongside the day's Bible reading? Rembrandt's *Return of the Prodigal*, for instance, takes us into a portrayal of an intimate embrace with a loving Father that any age can understand. Using this picture as a basis for discussion, meditation or confession puts the worship in touch with a deeper spirituality and draws on the very best that we as humans have to offer. After discussing the story and the different characters in the painting, invite someone to 'become' the father, the prodigal son or the elder brother in a 'hot-seating' exercise. This spontaneous drama brings the story and the characters to life and age is no barrier to taking part, whether in the hot seat or asking the questions.

Is there someone in your church with artistic gifts who could create pictures just for your church or take on the responsibility of finding pictures to enhance the theme of your service? Are there people who could deploy their technological gifts to use these pictures in a computer slideshow accompanied by music as an aid to meditation?

Mothering Sunday active prayers

Lastly, as an example of prayers that draw on more than just words, here's a selection of prayers for Mothering Sunday—a day when churches are especially likely to have all ages present in the service.

These 'active prayers' involve seeing, smelling, touching and tasting. Each prayer takes place at a special 'station' set up beforehand. Make sure there is enough room for several people to stand around each one. Are they pushchair- and wheelchair-friendly, too? You may or may not choose to display the Bible verses, depending on how literate your congregation is.

Describe briefly what each station entails, and invite every-one to visit the stations and pray at each one in different ways. Put on some quiet music. It can be helpful to prime one or two people to get things moving if your congregation doesn't usually leave their seats. Draw the prayers to a close by saying the Lord's Prayer when almost everyone has returned to their seat. Of course, you can adapt the stations to make them appropriate for your context (setting up more or fewer, varying the activities and so on).

Station 1: Confessing when we don't treat our families well

- From the Bible: 'Honour your father and your mother' (Exodus 20:12a).
- Have a large picture of a house showing the different rooms inside. Place a pile of cut-out heart shapes next to the picture. Print out the following:

'Think about your home or the home where you grew up. Which room (or memory) would you really like God's love to fill? Where do/did you have most quarrels or fights with your family or friends? Tell God how sorry you are for your part in these troubles and place a heart in the relevant room to ask him to heal the memory and fill it with his love in the future.'

Station 2: Giving thanks for our mothers

- From the Bible: 'A wife of noble character who can find? She is worth far more than rubies... She watches over the affairs of her household and does not eat the bread of idleness. Her children arise and call her blessed; her husband also, and he praises her: "Many women do noble things, but you surpass them all"' (Proverbs 31:10, 27–29).

• Have a pile of paste jewels (available from craft shops) and a treasure chest. Print out the following:

'Our mothers and grandmothers have done things for us that shine like jewels. What is the most precious thing they've done for you? Say thank you to God for that precious thing and place a gem in the treasure chest to show how valuable it is to you.'

Station 3: Giving thanks for the mothering of the church we belong to

• From the Bible: 'Praise be to the God and Father of our Lord Jesus Christ, the Father of compassion and the God of all our comfort, who comforts us in all our troubles, so that we can comfort those in any trouble with the comfort we ourselves have received from God' (2 Corinthians 1:3–4).

• Have some soft pieces of cloth and blanket washed with the well-known fabric softener. Have a minimum amount of liquid in the bottle and place it in the middle of the table with the lid off. Print out the following:

'Hold the soft cloth, smell it and give thanks to God for the way the people in your church care for you and comfort you when you need comfort. Who do you thank him for particularly?'

Station 4: Praying for the motherless and the childless

- From the Bible: 'Don't call me Naomi… Call me Mara, because the Almighty has made my life very bitter' (Ruth 1:20). 'You must help needy orphans and widows' (James 1:27b, CEV).
- Have paper in the shape of teardrops, pens, some segments of lemon, a basket and a bin. Print out the following:

'Taste the lemon, write in the teardrop shape how it tastes to you and leave the paper in a basket on the table. For many people, there is a lot of bitterness tied up with motherhood and childhood. Pray for those people while you still have that bitter taste in your mouth.'

Station 5: Committing ourselves to caring for others

- From the Bible: 'But when [Moses' mother] could hide him no longer, she got a papyrus basket for him and coated it with tar and pitch. Then she placed the child in it and put it among the reeds along the bank of the Nile' (Exodus 2:3).

- Have a Moses basket, some slips of cream-coloured paper or papyrus-like paper (from craft shops) and some black pens, and a poster suggesting various ways of showing care for people: a smile, a phone call, some time over a coffee, a big hug, a lift somewhere, giving blood, donating money to a charity, buying some Fairtrade goods, or sponsoring a child in a developing country. Print out the following:

'Ask God who he would like you to care for this week. Write their name and how you're going to show God's care for them on a piece of "papyrus" and place it in the Moses basket, just as Moses' mother took care of Moses by putting him in a place of safety. Commit yourself to care for that person in that way. When you've actually done it, you can take the papyrus out of the Moses basket. Perhaps you could set yourself the challenge of achieving it by next week?'

In my experience, prayer at stations like this can work well, with everyone taking part, praying at their own pace, making the most of the opportunity to take responsibility for praying very seriously. However, if prayer stations are used too often and in too similar a way each time, they can appear a 'cheap' or 'thoughtless' way of praying—as if the leader can't be bothered to prepare decent intercessions, so he's just put out a table with some matchsticks on it. On the other hand, a Messy Church colleague has successfully used stations during a service with 250 people of different ages present.

Use story

As we explore what church is for and how to be church as effectively as possible, it becomes apparent that story is of great importance—above all, the story of what God has done in Jesus, but also the story of what he is doing in our lives (which we'll come to a bit later in this chapter). Anglicans say at the start of a service that they have come to 'hear and receive his Holy Word'. The people of God come together to remind themselves of God's story, just as the believers did in the early Church, so that our faith is centred on Jesus and all he has done.

If we've been Christians for ages, we need to be reminded of the timeless stories of who Jesus is and what he did, to keep our faith refreshed and firmly grounded in him and to inspire us to live lives more like his. If we have been Christians for only a short time, we need to hear these stories and have the chance to think through them and learn from them. That way, our faith will be modelled on Jesus, the best inspiration ever of someone who loves God and loves other people, a man who is completely like us, yet also completely 'other'— our God who lived on earth 2000 years ago and still lives and works now, through his Spirit and through his people.

Sermons can be glorious, of course, and preaching has worked miracles throughout the Old and New Testaments and beyond. The prophets preached; Jesus preached; Paul and Peter preached. There will always be a key place for it. Preaching is a great low-tech, controllable and, in many ways, easy way to teach, but I am not convinced that it is the most effective way to learn or to hear God's voice when all ages are present.

Leaving aside the actual content for a moment, a sermon is an obvious means of communication, as it can be delivered to many people at the same time, doesn't require anything more than a loud voice in the delivery and is predictable in terms of timing. It is also non-threatening in the sense that no one except the preacher is expected to respond openly during it, and he or she is guaranteed a captive audience. This is a very good thing for hard-pressed ministers with too much to do, and for people who learn best by listening or people who need to sit and observe rather than risk taking part.

Given that human beings enjoy and remember stories so well, though, should we not at least consider giving story a more pre-eminent place in our gathered worship than it has enjoyed over recent years? Story is something that all ages can enjoy and learn from at many different levels. Are we willing to put in as much preparation to telling and exploring a story as into preparing a sermon? Or will it just be muttered out during the Gospel reading by someone with their head in the book and their mind on Sunday lunch?

We might think that storytelling is simply entertainment, but, taken seriously, scriptural storytelling goes far beyond that and can become the sacred space where God's word is allowed to interact with our own experience, transforming lives. Done well, it is a brilliant basis for building up community: it is enjoyable and engaging and it creates a safe space, a relationship between storyteller and listeners, and between the listeners through shared experience. Stories can play their part in healing on an individual or corporate level. Keith White writes:

It is one of the most important of tasks for Christian families and the church, at times of worship, to tell and retell and celebrate these

stories in their ruggedness and context. At the same time, through
fellowship and prayer, it is vital to create the context in which
children can bring their real concerns, suffering and fears into the
open and connect them to the revelation of God's story.[15]

The Godly Play approach, which has been used in the United States since 1972 and has proved effective in the UK more recently, has led to a revival in the respect paid to 'story' as a means of coming close to God and to each other. Through these reflective stories, with their emphasis on response through 'wondering' together in a safe community space, practitioners have seen children and adults encountering story in a dynamic and Spirit-filled way, being given the chance to question and listen to what God and others are saying.

Other storytelling styles can appeal to different learning preferences, to the imagination and the soul as well as the mind. There are many resources to draw on, such as the almost rhetorical style of 'response stories', in which the listeners respond to key words or phrases with a set response in words and/or actions. In the verse version of 'The house on the rock' from the BRF *Barnabas* website, people go away humming the chorus and practising the hand actions as the story settles into their long-term memory.[16]

On *Barnabas* RE Days we sometimes tell a dramatised version of 'The good Samaritan' that involves the group creating the very scenery of the story, the different characters walking down a road, robbers leaping out and innkeepers offering hospitality. It's a spontaneous unrehearsed version that appeals to kinaesthetic learners (those who learn best by 'doing') and visual learners.

A simple prop that 'might have belonged' to a character in a story can fill it out for the imagination. Picture what you could include in Mary and Joseph's suitcase as they set out to Bethlehem, or in a briefcase belonging to the rich young ruler.

A story told from a character's viewpoint rather than in third-person narrative can help to develop an interest in and empathy for this individual, which in turn builds a bridge between the story and our 21st-century lives as we see where the character's feelings and experiences chime in with ours. Time and time again, we have seen the story of the man with leprosy (Mark 1:40–42) change from a story to a challenge and inspiration for our lives when it is told from the point of view of the man with leprosy himself. I heard a recent 'sermon slot' on the feeding of the 5000 (John 6:1–13) that was wholly taken up with a first-person account from the boy in the story, now grown up and in prison for his faith. The story held as much theology and challenge as any sermon.

These are just a handful of ways to help bring a story to life so that people of all ages can engage with God's word.

In Messy Church we don't have time for added extras: the whole two-hour session is the service but the actual celebration lasts only about 15 minutes, and we have found that it is more engaging to focus on story than on sermon or 'talk'. We try to share the story in such a way that it works on both the imagination and the intellect, settling into the listener's heart, shaping the pattern of who they are and the life decisions they make.

Include participation

It has long been recognised in churches that a good way to keep young people involved is to use them, to give them something to do in a service—make them altar boys or choir girls, or give them the privileged job of handing out hymn books or lighting the candles. Although it often 'works' in the sense that children like to have a job to do (unlike adults, who usually flee commitment at pathological speed), I am slightly uneasy about the need behind this practice, because it feels as if we are giving children something to do to keep them busy rather than because a job actually needs doing. Also, perhaps we need to do it because what goes on in church may be so boring to young people that even waiting for a collection plate to do the rounds seems nail-bitingly gripping by comparison. Church must be able to offer more than this!

Paul Butler, the Bishop of Southampton, writes in his 2007 Lent talks (published on the Diocese of Winchester website):

We need to see children as equal worshippers when we gather together for worship. Our regular worship needs to be one in which children are expected to participate, and whose contribution is valued. This must have implications for every aspect of our worship, but particularly for the feel and ethos that we create.

'Participation' is a key word here. We have learned passivity in many churches and, while shared leadership is increasing, there is still often a default setting of 'sit and be done to' in a service. A service needs good leadership, keeping it moving and responding sensitively to what happens, but can we not let go of the assumption that only the elite few are qualified to play an active and responsible role in the service? It's interesting that one of the many 'messes' we're learning about in Messy Church is the mess of relinquishing control—letting go and allowing people to do just what they want to do rather than dictating to them what they should be doing at what moment and with whom. I'm sure it's all terribly postmodern, or post-postmodern or pre-ancient or something, but it seems to be true that these days many people are suspicious of authority and respond well to being given responsibility for their own actions.

Another messiness we're learning about is the power of God working on the messy edges, where he hasn't been organised out of the picture. It seems to be the place where the exciting encounters happen, just as the least likely people can be the ones who come up with a shining insight.

Participation is about inviting everyone to engage with different elements of the service in a way that makes them comfortable but sometimes gently takes them out of that comfort zone to a place of challenge. Consider for a moment, say, the men in your church. What do they do five days a week? The list for my church would read something like: keeping the computers for an international company running smoothly; supervising all shipping in the Solent; teaching people to drive; driving patients to and from hospital; business management in London; gardening; visiting ill friends and taking the elderly shopping; teaching music; building. Through the week, these men do active, responsible jobs. Sunday comes and the most they are asked to do is to run the digital projector or make the coffee. Otherwise they just sit back for an hour and passively listen. We could argue that at least they're getting some well-earned time off. We could also argue that Sunday—and, by extension, God—is thereby completely disjointed from the rest of their life and the interplay between the two is minimised.

It's worth thinking through the different elements of your time of worship to see if any or all can be made more participative, to include more people. Instead of bringing a few church members out to the front to illustrate a story, are there some sound effects or visuals that the whole church could provide? If questions are being asked, could people get into groups to answer them so that more voices are heard? When prayers are being offered, what could everyone say responsively or do individually as part of that time? When the Bible is being read, will it be more memorable if it is read together or perhaps divided up so that different parts of the church have different roles in the dialogue?

The shorthand question is: who, apart from the minister, is actively bringing something to offer to God and his people in this act of worship?

Deciding to design a service that invites people to 'do', to participate, rather than to sit like sponges soaking up teaching, can change the whole course of your planning. The teenage leaders of the Dronfield Messy Church read the suggestions in my book *Messy Church* for a celebration on the theme of light and decided they were rubbish! They decided that a much more effective activity would be to lead everyone blindfold around the church to feel what it's like to try to go forward in the dark. Our own Messy Church team thought this was such a good idea that we did the same in our session on 'Guidance'. We found that letting people do it themselves meant that they came out with some heartfelt and original responses to the activity rather than absorbing what we thought they should learn from it. We learned from them.

At the very heart of a church that wants to grow and change, there needs to be an attitude of listening to 'people on the edge'. A church needs to be humble enough to include some unlikely groups in its planning and decision-making at all levels: sympathetic non-attending husbands of women who belong to church, teenagers, children (when time restraints permit), people with special needs or those who will speak up for them. The very core of a church should involve its members, of all kinds, in taking part. In an article in the *Church Times*, Jonathan Bartley argues that one reason for the churches' conspicuous lack of ability to deliver all-age worship is that children are not included in the decision-making of the church:

The exclusion [of children] from the main 'corporate' meeting is routine and institutionalised across all ages... The reason is that children have also been conspicuous by their absence in consultation and decision-making. And it's a crying shame, because children can often ask the most simple, but also the most profound, questions that adults are afraid to ask.[17]

One church denomination systematically denies anyone under the age of 16 the right to serve on the governing body of the local church, while permitting anyone up to the age of 116 and beyond to continue to serve on it.

Think of the 14-year-olds you know. Should the restriction mentioned above be reviewed? What changes would need to be made to encourage younger people to participate in the church's governing body? How many young people have a say in the way your church is run? Ask the same question of the other discrete groups that make up your church, such as the elderly, single people, those with mental or physical disabilities, young marrieds, or those from overseas.

Use invitation

Invitation is a very important touchstone for all-age worship. In a church service, my toes curled up when I heard the leader barking, 'I want *all* the children up at the front. Come on now! I know there are more children than this here today. Where are you? Come on, we haven't got all day.'

On the one hand, this is an attempt to make the children feel valued and important, and I humbly applaud the good intention behind such an attempt. On the other hand, it assumes that all children like to be put on display, something which is simply not true. It leaves the children no choice, as the option of staying in their seats or in the play area now becomes rudeness towards the leader. It also assumes that the children are the only ones in church who enjoy being up at the front—and dragging children out to perform a task that could better be done by an easel ('Now hold this placard up for me') or that insults the intelligence of the average two-year-old ('Who can tell me what this is?') comes under the category of finding rubbish for idle hands to do. We can do better than this!

In primary schools, you will often see unsupervised children setting up the assembly space—moving benches, finding and playing CDs, making sure the audiovisual equipment is set out and ready and focal tables are in place. These are 'real' jobs that actually need doing and require a degree of responsibility. In a church service, there will be more ownership if all sorts of people have been involved in the setting up, so there is no reason why the teenagers shouldn't set up the digital projector or arrange flowers, why the children shouldn't help with the sound equipment or do sidesperson's duties, handing out books, welcoming people and finding seats for them. During the service itself we can invite 'anyone who would like...' to help, rather than saying, 'I need a child to help' when there are jobs that need doing, like lighting candles, carrying objects up in procession, reading a part in a script or offering answers to a question. This is more appropriate than insisting that only children should have the opportunity to take part.

An invitation to respond to questions in a service is important, too. Questions can be a great tool for encouraging participation but they need to be handled with care. Quite apart from the closed questions with right or wrong answers ('What is an ephod?' 'How many disciples does this passage mention?' 'Who walked on water?'), we need a respectful attitude behind more personal questions, whether they are addressed to children or adults. At one service, the minister brought all the children to the front and asked them, 'What are you worried about?' Imagine for a moment that *you* had been asked to answer that question publicly. How would you feel? Would you want to answer honestly? Would the minister have asked the same question of the CEO of a large business or a husband whose marriage was known to be in difficulties?

One of the children in this instance offered the answer, 'Spanish.' The minister, not quite sure what to make of this, laughed, encouraged the congregation to laugh by agreeing in a slightly facetious way that homework was a worry, and moved on to the next child. Quite apart from the fact that homework can be a genuine worry for many young people, and that worry had been undervalued and dismissed by the patronising response of the whole church, after the service the child explained that what he was worried about was the situation in Spain where terrorists had just blown up a train, killing hundreds of people. This was something indeed to be concerned about.

We need to give respect to everyone we encounter, not just those who demand it vociferously. Questions can be open-ended rather than closed: 'How might Peter have been feeling at this moment?' 'I wonder when you last met someone who was hurting inside?' 'What do you think is the most exciting part of this story?' A response to answers given might be a simple word of thanks, a reflection back of the answer given ('She was overjoyed; mmmm') or an indication that you have really listened to the answer ('A cow? I've never thought of that before'). Any of these responses respects the fact that the person answering may be considering the issue from a different but equally valid viewpoint to your own.

Be real

There are two ways of understanding the importance of being real in our churches. The most important way is to understand that, as individuals and as a community, we will grow best by having wholesome, inspiring, *real* models of discipleship around us. We need people who are real about their faith and whose faith is real, to inspire us by their behaviour and witness. We need to see a fellow member of the church asking for prayer at a tough time in life, so that when we're going through a similar time, we know we can ask for prayer ourselves. There was a case in the news of a nurse who was disciplined after she had offered to pray for a patient: we need to hear stories like this of how other Christians are living out their faith in their workplaces, to inspire and challenge us in our own situations.

A church of people who need to pretend that everything is fine, and are not in the habit of sharing what is happening for good or ill in their home, school or workplace, may well develop into a community where children grow up assuming, because no one there talks about work, politics, films, illness, finance, marriage break-up, the Internet, addiction, triumphs, anniversaries or school, that church and therefore God have no relevance to these other parts of life. Here is another good reason for being an all-age community: our children need to grow up surrounded by 'storybook Christians' who are teenagers, young adults and older adults—in other words, Christians whose lives tell the story of Jesus in their actions, reactions, words and decisions. In fact, Christians need this at every different stage of life, not just during childhood.

The second aspect of reality in worship is an extension of what we have already explored about storytelling and about being as participatory as possible. It is the way that we should bring everyday reality into our Sunday worship. As we have seen, there is always a danger that we box off our six-days-a-week life from our Sunday worship: we behave as if God belongs solely in church, and work belongs solely in the office/school/home. If worship is to be genuine and honest, we need to bring the messiness of the world around us into contact with the healing truth of scripture. As Keith White writes, 'Children who are fully part of the worshipping community will find themselves constantly in touch with the fragility and messiness of life and the forces of evil and darkness, while at the same time being reassured by God's faithfulness, mercy and grace.'[18]

If Sunday worship was seen more as a practice ground for being close to God and having him close to us in our workplaces and our homes, we would have a more integrated faith, based on the reality of a God who is concerned as much about how we treat members of our department on a Monday as the way we approach Communion on a Sunday. If preaching is about taking the gospel truths and apply-ing them to life today, we should be hearing each other's stories, both the encouraging and the despairing ones.

The God who chose to become a chippy is at much at home in a scruffy modern staffroom as in a soaring medieval building. Church isn't a temple: *we* are the new temples of the Holy Spirit as Paul describes us in 1 Corinthians 6:19. We are the places where people can meet God, places that are full of the glory of his presence and where the carpentry that matters isn't on the woodwormy beams but on what holds our lives together. The extraordinary God lives in ultra-ordinary people in their ordinary homes, workplaces and schools, and we need to help everyone recognise him in those places and be reassured and challenged that he is there with them and through them. Even after five years, my Junior Church group find it strange to think that God is at school with them: they need a great deal of persuasion to mention school life in prayers. The divorce between life and church life begins very early.

So let's hear what God is doing in people's work lives. Let's have a testimony at the drop of a hat; let's make any excuse for hearing each other's stories. Let's bring objects from work and school into church to talk about. Let's have pictures of those places and people to pray for. Let's pray as often for the leaders of local businesses as for the church leaders, as often for school teachers as for Sunday school teachers.

Let's also bring real issues into church—stories from the news, of course, but also an acknowledgment of the worlds of media, sport and global issues, which have so much influence on the lives of many in our churches. Let's learn to reflect on these issues critically and become equipped to discuss them outside church.

This consideration of being real leads on to the wider question of how we equip people of all ages to practise their faith outside church—not just in the workplace but in *homes* throughout the week, with adults learning alongside children. When do we make time to meet with other parents and grandparents to discuss what Bible storytelling resources we've discovered for bedtime? Could we find a context in which to share the ways we pray with our children? How do we say grace before a meal? How do we talk about God with children? Grandparents can have a huge reservoir of resources and ideas to draw on: let's remember this and celebrate the church's unique status as the family of God—the extended family of God across all ages and across all countries and cultures.

Kate Kendall told me about an all-age service that she and her husband Giles began in St Mary's Church, Sawston, near Cambridge. It's called Open Door and is based on the principle that everyone is involved because Jesus involves everyone. Regular members are asked to make coffee, be welcomers, join the music group or join a rota to lead activities aimed at a particular age group, and leaders are limited to doing their job once every half-term to avoid burn-out. Overall, Kate describes it as working more like a collective than a traditional church service:

We start with three worship songs led on keyboard and guitars, and displayed on a screen; then the younger children's group goes to the vestry for their activity. The adults/older children have a drama or game, the Bible reading and a talk and then we have reflective prayers written by one of our congregation. Then there are standard prayers—a simple confession, the Lord's Prayer, another song and an offertory prayer and the younger group come back in to share what they've done. Then we might share bread and wine (consecrated at an earlier service) or say the grace together and a final song and that's it.

Our advice to anyone?

- *If you value all-age, then go for it. What have you got to lose?*
- *Be genuine—people spot a fake and will avoid you. So, if you don't value all-age, be honest and stick to what you're good at.*
- *Be relaxed—people want to feel comfortable when they come to church.*
- *Have a comfortable families' area (not 'children's corner') in church with high-quality toys that you'd have at home—not tat from a jumble sale.*
- *Run all-age weekly in term time, so families know that if it's a school week it's also a church week, rather than having to work out if it's a first Sunday, second Sunday etc. Who on earth thinks like that apart from churchy types?*
- *Devise a service where the minister is the facilitator, not the person who has to carry the whole thing.*

What aspects of Open Door could you usefully learn from?

Conclusion

All-age worship is challenging and difficult. There are touch-stones that we can apply, but more depends on the spirit in which we live and work and have our being than on the mechanics. Much depends on the awareness and attitude of the leaders, and on the understanding and appreciation of the bigger picture by every member of the church. It's not just what you do; it's the way that you do it. Similarly, the service depends on the attitude of church members, and some of these will need careful preparation for anything that is trying to be genuinely all-age.

Church leaders need support to do this very demanding job and it's unlikely that they will be able to sustain change without the support of the church leadership teams. Perhaps, for some churches, it will be more appropriate to introduce very small changes that reflect an attitude of welcoming all ages. For example, an hour's training with the welcome team, which focuses on the needs of different age groups as they come into a church service, might introduce some different ideas.

Perhaps you know you would be fighting a losing battle to make every service in your church fully all-age. You may decide to change one service just once a month or to start a new all-age service at a different time, which allows those who prefer segregated services to carry on as they always have done. It is important to realise that, for many church congregations, the idea of being all-age is in complete opposition to everything they have been brought up to practise. It is new, revolutionary, uncharted and threatening, so it behoves anyone wanting to make changes to tread gently and not to expect too much too soon.

So is there a painless way to leap across the gulf between old and new? Perhaps not, but the next chapter introduces some ideas about bridges between traditional and pioneering ways of being church.

＊

– Chapter 5 –

Coping with change

You may have read through the ideas in the previous chapter with ever-increasing despondency. 'Yes, but the thought of asking my 10.30 congregation to do something as radical as moving from their seats to a prayer station during a service sends cold shivers down my spine. The outrage it would be met with! The silent refusal to leave "my pew that I've sat in for the last 53 years". The muttering over coffee of "Is this the country we fought and died for?" And as for joining in a story with actions—I might as well ask the congregation to take their clothes off and hula-dance down the nave.'

I try to think that this sort of refusal to change belongs only in my imagination and that churches have moved on from an entrenched 'I do it my way' attitude. In the course of its work, however, the *Barnabas* ministry team meets ministers and children's leaders across the UK who have to cope with similar attitudes on a daily basis, not from comic-book stereotypes of Christians but from lovable, sincere, long-standing members of churches who have faithfully supported their congregation in prayer, time and money over many years. We have also met frustrated church members whose ministers are nervous about trying something new or have no time or energy to support changes.

Sometimes the refusal to consider change comes from members of a church whose traditional services are providing exactly what people need. They celebrate Jesus in the midst of them. The services are attracting new members. They balance dignified formality with genuine love and good teaching. They provide a changelessness, reliability and constancy that take on a symbolic status in a rapidly changing world. The people in these services have learnt that church is a safe space for them and for the friends that they invite to join them.

I hate to say it, but I really believe that a minister will only achieve misunderstandings, hurt and outrage, with church members leaving in umbrage, if they try to lead such a congregation down a radically new and different path, be that all-age or something else. The changes they are allowed to make will be so cosmetic that they will appear to encourage hypocrisy. It's a 'new wine into old wineskins' scenario: it takes such a fundamental shift in understanding to appreciate why a church should make a genuine effort to be all-age that a half-hearted, ill-considered approach can result only in old wineskins disintegrating and the new wine dribbling away. It's no use paying lip service to the all-age ideal: an established church needs to be totally honest with itself and commit itself to putting self last and God and others first if it wants to go down this track. Otherwise it's better not to go there. It's such a challenge and so alien to the way we have done church in this country for centuries that such a decision cannot be taken lightly.

It goes against the grain but, realistically, unless you belong to a church of radiantly saintly, selfless Christians with no hang-ups, I have to advocate a fresh start for a church, minister or group considering all-age worship. With a fresh start, they can ask, 'How can we be a community with Christ at the centre which makes it possible for all people to follow Jesus?' They can decide right from the word 'go' that the worshipping community will be open to learning from every new group and individual that comes into it: it will be shaped by outsiders as much as by its own traditions. One of the reasons Messy Church has fitted more or less joyfully into our church life is because we haven't asked any of the established Sunday congregations to give up 'what they like' on a Sunday in order to accommodate people of different ages, backgrounds and stages of faith. Messy Church happens separately on a Thursday evening, so that nobody's cherished Sunday services are affected. It's a 'both/and' rather than an 'either/or' situation.

This doesn't mean that any church can't usefully use any of the ideas in the wonderful range of all-age worship books available. Perhaps, in your situation, they might serve a different purpose, gently introducing your church to some different possibilities in worship even if there is no one present under the age of 65. Perhaps they might serve to loosen some of the fixed attitudes that make it so hard to change styles of worship. Maybe the church, ten years from now, will reap the benefits of what you have tactfully sown in your area. But the attitude underlying an all-age church—a respect for and willingness to learn from outsiders—can be brought into play in any church, even if nothing overtly all-age is actually done.

Of course, the problem for many hard-pressed ministers is that they simply don't have time to add anything new into the diary. It was refreshing to hear one vicar, visiting Messy Church with a group of his leaders, saying, 'Yes, we're interested, but if we do Messy Church, we need to decide first what's going to go. We can't just keep on adding more to what we do.'

The challenge for the wider Church is to take the all-age question seriously and, at the very least, ask rigorous questions before a pioneer church or a fresh expression begins. Will the new venture be fresh in its welcome and acceptance of all ages? If the answer is 'no', so be it. A Tuesday lunchtime gathering knows for sure that it won't have anyone there between the ages of five and 16, and a church that meets at three in the morning to welcome clubbers can hardly expect many eight-year-olds to burst through the doors. But the rest of us need to flag up these questions at the very start of our deliberations about direction and purpose: if we want to be the best church possible for all who belong to it, can we be so *without* all ages present? And if we are blessed enough to have all ages present, how are we going to use that fact to God's advantage and our own?

The good news is that, at the moment, there is an amazing amount of freedom in the Church to risk doing something new, and there is more support than ever before as we tentatively walk the new path that we feel God is calling us down. There are countrywide examples of fresh expressions to read about, be inspired by and learn from. There is a call to be flexible, even in matters that have traditionally been non-negotiable for some groups, like the liturgy of the Anglican Communion service. With this caring, careful yet generous context, congregations in the UK are better placed than at perhaps any other time in church history to have our grassroots inspiration taken seriously and supported. Pioneer ministry is recognised, respected and welcomed, and what could be more pioneering than re-evaluating our whole approach to how we relate to children in the church?

Human beings are such creatures of habit: within a few months... no, within a few *weeks* of something new beginning, expectations will be established that will take earthquakes, tornadoes, flood and fire to remove. I find it intriguing that so many fresh expressions have thought creatively and imaginatively about the setting and style of their worship, but have automatically assumed that if children appear, the only option is to turf them out to some form of Sunday school. It may not be given that name, and the activities will be jolly and child-friendly, but the message will be, once again, that it is inappropriate for children to be part of the worshipping community. Fresh expressions, though, are the perfect opportunity to put everything into the melting pot—to dream dreams and see visions, to take risks and meet the God who works on the edges with those who are marginalised.

Whether we are creating a totally new expression of church or holding a different service that is part of an existing church's ministry, an important aspect of the whole process of change comes back to relationships again. In an ideal world, you don't want anyone to feel threatened by the developments you're considering nor do you want them to feel competitive, rejected, second-best, superior, out of touch, unloved or on the shelf. You do want as many people as possible to feel part of what is going on, committed to it in love, prayer, time and money, interested in what happens and encouraged by what God is doing through their church, even if they don't set foot in the new service themselves.

To this end, there are several issues to bear in mind.

Building up trust

The leadership of a church needs to make new thoughts and plans known to as many people as possible, as informally as possible. Chatting through proposals over a cup of tea is less confrontational than bringing them up in a formal setting, which runs the risk of backing people into a corner. Listening is as important as sharing the plans.

Discerning unexpected gifts

God puts people with appropriate gifts into a church at the right time. A new project can bring some surprising gifts to the surface, gifts that haven't been evident before. How else would we have found out that one elderly member of our congregation spins wool or that one of the younger members is particularly good at enabling others to do art? It is vital that a team is open to spotting gifts in the least likely people, helps to share the workload involved in beginning something new, and also spreads the commitment to the new project into unexpected byways of the whole church. Several of our male Messy Church leaders have been drawn in because of their 'friend of a friend' relationships with other church members. Who would have known that one husband would come ready-armed with a Certificate in Basic Food Hygiene and a cool military approach to mass catering? How would we have mobilised the baking skills of the Mothers' Union if someone more imaginative than I hadn't taken the responsibility of waxing lyrical to them about the mission field of Messy Church?

Including everyone from the very start

How are you going to listen to everyone, including the children, right from the inception of the planning process? A diocesan official explained to me recently that a large 'successful' church in his diocese wouldn't contemplate an all-age approach: 'If you asked children and parents in that church what they want, they would all say that they want children to go out to their groups, because that's all they've ever known. It's the only model of church they recognise. They've never seen an alternative pattern.'

Simply asking what people want isn't going to elicit more than a jazzed-up version of what they know. Instead, try to find out more specifically:

- which parts of a service help them feel closest to God.
- how church could best help them with being a Christian at school, work or at home.
- what gifts they feel they have that could be used in an all-age church.
- what would encourage them to invite their friends along.

Communications

As the plans progress, the importance of more formal communications grows—the parish magazine, the notices, the posters, the emails rejoicing in developments and bewailing hiccups. We would have had far more helpers early on in Messy Church if we had opened up our thoughts to a wider cross-section of the Sunday congregations.

Even now, we need to do far more to keep Messy Church in the eye of the Sunday church. The PCC has suggested a Messy Church Sunday, when each of the congregations is given an update on what is happening there and a taste of what we do. It has encouraged us to have a freestanding display board within the church building so that it becomes more of a fixture among the church's wider family. Communications are crucial to keep everyone in touch with what is going on.

Language

The way you view the new project will be very apparent to people from the language that you use and allow to be used to describe it. If it's church, don't let anyone get away with calling it anything but church. 'Everyone at church and people who come on Thursdays too' means that people who come on Thursdays aren't part of the church. Avoid anything that smacks of hierarchy: it is very easy for anything at which children are present to be labelled exclusively 'children's church' or 'your club for children', to be looked down on and treated as less than the 'real thing'. Part of the reason for the name 'Messy Church' is to set the bar high in terms of expectations. It isn't a club but a church that expresses itself in an unconventional way.

Once we have set change in motion—and, all being well, got as many church members on board as possible—we should remember that a 'new project', 'new church' or 'new wine' does not necessarily mean that all the riches of our Christian tradition are automatically thrown out. As a church sacrificially puts everything into God's hands to be re-evaluated, it is liberated to try some different ways of worshipping together. Working with all ages can be a chance to revisit or encounter for the first time some of the aspects of discipleship and worship that have helped Christians grow closer to God over the centuries. One way of helping people to come to terms with change in a church is to build bridges between ancient traditions and today's practices.

Images

How many times have we visited cathedrals and heard that the stained-glass windows were the way that a medieval non-literate congregation would 'read' the Christian story? While I have my doubts about this (it's very hard to pick out specific stories or distinguish one bearded character from another without the aid of a guide book and binoculars), I don't doubt that images, pictures, films and icons can be as powerful today as they have ever been in helping people to encounter and go deeper with God. It can be very refreshing to be given time and space to get inside the skin of a great piece of art, as we saw in Chapter 4. Artists ask questions and challenge us to explore a dimension in which words aren't enough. Art will speak to different people in different ways, and older people have no advantage in interpreting it. Throughout the centuries, Christians have used icons to come closer to God. As we move on in our Christian journey together, it might be a reassurance to some to encounter traditional art as well as modern depictions of Jesus.

Meditation

Again, here is a practice that has benefited Christians for centuries. It is coming into classrooms in primary schools more and more (although not necessarily in the form of Christian meditation). This shows that we don't need to shy away from including quieter, more meditative moments in our worship when children are present. The deep silence of a carefully prepared meditation on scripture can speak as loudly to a child or adult as can a three-point sermon. We recently included a time of quiet to 'tune into God' during a Messy Church celebration. When it was introduced, I have to admit, my heart sank as I thought of the glue-sloshing, nail-hammering, junk-modelling chaos we'd just been creating so joyfully together—but, although we had babies and toddlers as well as older children and relatively unchurched people present, the short silence was profound and significant. I'm not sure how God spoke to everyone else, but perhaps he was telling me something about trust and letting go of control.

Is there someone in your church who has experience of, for example, using the Jesus Prayer? Could they share this with the rest of the church? If a style of worship is explained and introduced carefully, and if children can sense that what they are invited to join is genuine, they are no more likely to behave inappropriately than adults!

Liturgy

Liturgy, the set of formularies for public worship, inevitably has a certain formality, but, if it goes too far beyond 'the ordinary' altogether or elevates the extraordinary at the expense of the ordinary, it risks losing touch with a worship that extends into all seven days of the week. Used exclusively, it becomes a set of rituals with no links to the workplace, the home or the school where Christians are painfully trying to live out their discipleship. It tucks church neatly into a sealed box so that it can have no influence on the other parts of our lives. We need a language that can express the sacred in the ordinary and the ordinary in the sacred if we are to have a grounded and genuine expression of our faith. We need a language that reflects and reflects on our life today.

But all-age worship doesn't have to abandon all formula, ritual or any kind of liturgy in an attempt to be relevant and meaningful to people at different stages of faith and life. The liturgies of the Iona Community, for example, take ancient patterns of prayer, such as the Advent Antiphons, and create new words on the old structures. There is resonance from the old form and an almost shocking power as the incongruity of the new is heard.

The Northumbria Community makes a point of including archaic language as a bridge with the past. The description of their daily offices includes the following statement: 'Midday Prayer retains the "thee" and "thou" forms of speech. This may seem unfamiliar to the many who are used only to modern language, but it is a deliberate attempt to highlight the contemporary relevance of the treasure of prayer from long ago.'[19] The resources of the Iona and Northumbria Communities are available in published form for general use.[20]

Although it isn't possible for every congregation to develop its own specific liturgy, appropriate to its own people (and some denominations don't give permission for this to happen), it is well worth revitalising potentially tired and predictable liturgies, with some very short and easy approaches, used perhaps on just one part of the service each week. If nothing else, an occasional question will give everyone the opportunity to look at one part of the service in a slightly different way. In an ideal world, you would have a day together to think through questions like these in depth in an informal workshop setting, but not many of us can do that in any sustainable way, so perhaps it's best to start with short, manageable challenges included in the service itself. For example:

- Why do you think we always say this greeting at the start of the service?
- This part of the service reminds us why we're here. There are lots of reasons mentioned: I wonder which one is special to you today?
- When you say this confession, what picture do you have in your mind of God?
- Who are we saying this part of the service to?
- We're going to say this together and afterwards I'm going to ask which was your favourite bit of it / which part you found puzzling / surprising / strange.
- Look at [Bible reference] in your Bibles. Let's say this part of our service by reading it from the Bible instead of the service sheet (for example, the Lord's Prayer, a blessing or confession).
- Let's try gathering [at this point] in our building to say this part of the service. (For example, by the door for the welcome, at a window overlooking the street for intercessions, around the font for the confession, or around the Communion table for a blessing.)

Such gentle but deliberate 'pointing' during the service will serve the same purpose as theatre lighting: it will highlight, give light and shade, show old valuable things in a new light, and add focus and interest.

Music

Sometimes the music in all-age worship is equated solely with 'children's songs'. Oh dear! No wonder all-age worship has a bad name. Surely common sense tells us that if we're going to sing and make music, we should do so in a variety of styles, so that everyone in our mixed gathering can be challenged by discovering something new and find comfort in something familiar. We may be quick to get into a 'That song didn't do anything for me' mentality, but is this what worship is about?

A church service that springs from a never-failing stream of justice and righteousness (see below), from a community in which individual members seek justice for others rather than for themselves, will have a completely different attitude to music from one in which people 'like what they like' and treat church as little more than a *Songs of Praise* karaoke session.

We should be fighting not for ourselves but for each other, demanding that each group of people in the church has the chance to enjoy different styles of music. How can we demonstrate to one congregation the majesty and richness of language in some traditional hymns? How can we introduce another congregation to songs from a more modern source? How can we make music from Iona, Taizé or our link church in Africa accessible? While some people may automatically pour cold water on anything new, others may only need a few words of explanation about why something 'a bit different' has been chosen, for them to adopt a more gracious attitude.

Music does raise temperatures like nothing else, perhaps because it can be such a powerful medium. Let's not even rehearse the tedious arguments about organ versus guitar: neither instrument is intrinsically holy; neither is better or worse for all-age worship than the other; both were met with hands raised in horror when they were first introduced into churches. Instead, let's encourage every sort of music, every available form, from CD to the recorder group, from exciting organ with all those fascinating stops and pedals to a three-year-old's energetic accompaniment to 'Shine, Jesus, shine' on maracas.

Avoid over-emphasis on performance: how many worship areas at the front of churches are so overrun with drum kits, keyboards, leads and pedals that the people at the front get lost in a forest of mic stands? Encourage and emphasise the concept of *serving* God and his people through music. This might include playing from the back of the congregation.

As we sit back and take a searching look at how we should express our worship to God in our all-age community, we have to ask, 'Are we going to sing at all?' Just because the people of God have always sung together, does that make it automatically right for us to do so? After all, where else in our Western 21st-century society do people sing? At football or rugby matches, in karaoke bars, in school assembly, perhaps, or around a campfire? Some people are members of choirs but communal singing is hardly something that most people do daily. A church set up to serve the needs of sportspeople in Cambridge has already decided that they will not sing, as it would be inappropriate for the particular people they hope to attract. Is singing together something that an all-age church should do?

Why do we sing songs and hymns, anyway? God evidently enjoys our worship through song, from Moses' and Miriam's song in Exodus 15 right on through the New Testament. Paul tells the Ephesians, 'Speak to one another with psalms, hymns and spiritual songs. Sing and make music in your heart to the Lord' (5:19).

Songs aren't an alternative to godly living, as the prophet Amos pointed out: 'Away with the noise of your songs! I will not listen to the music of your harps. But let justice roll on like a river, righteousness like a never-failing stream!' (Amos 5:23–24). Good songs can, however, give us a way to express the unsayable—all our love, praise, faith, trust, anger, doubt and hope summed up by this combination of words, music and silence. Using the songs of gifted composers can articulate something we have vaguely felt but been unable to put into words, which can be very liberating. The words to songs and hymns go with us out of the church service and into the rest of our lives, so that we find ourselves warbling songs of praise and verses of scripture over the washing-up or the photocopier. God can bring familiar songs to mind at unexpected times to remind us of his presence or of a particular truth that he's trying to get through to us.

Songs are a way of worshipping God together: singing is a participatory activity in which the individual is important but the sum of the parts is much more important. We make a much greater sound by singing together than by singing alone. Singing is also an activity that almost everyone can join in with, whatever their age. If people are unable to sing the words, they can still clap, dance, wiggle, worship with streamers or make a joyful noise with simple percussion instruments. At the other end of the spectrum, singing familiar songs and hymns means that people suffering from the early stages of dementia or those with cataracts can join in with the words they know by heart, rather than struggling to read them in a book or from a screen.

In a church with an all-age ethos, consider the following:

- *You believe in a variety of learning styles*, so use a variety of music styles. Be daring. Be unusual. Draw on the best of our wonderful Christian heritage, from plainchant to hip-hop. Ask different members of your church for input.
- *You believe in worshipping with the whole person*, so include times to listen to music as well as make it. Teach people how to be silent as well as loud.

- *You believe in the importance of the community as a whole and the value of coming together to worship God*, so consider changing references in some songs from 'I' to 'we'. It can make a huge difference.
- *You believe that everyone should be enabled to participate fully, regardless of age*, so if the words of a song are difficult to understand, consider unpacking a verse together or explaining the meaning of one word or story hidden in the song. If the words of a song are impossibly hard to get to grips with and yet still worth singing, consider adding some visuals—a projected image or someone expressing the song though dance or spontaneous painting. If a song is modern and potentially threatening to some by its very liveliness, draw out the way it uses scripture faithfully, links to your reading from the Bible for today, or corresponds to emotions expressed in the psalms or Gospels. Go to a primary school, find out how they display texts for young children to read easily and try displaying the song words in a similar way. While you're there, ask for a list of the songs the children sing in collective worship so that you can include them in your services. The repertoire of many primary schools extends a long way beyond 'All things bright and beautiful' and 'Give me oil in my lamp'.
- *You believe worship is something that overflows into everyday life*, so include some songs with easy-to-learn choruses and repetition that will stay in people's heads all week.

Ritual

Ritual is another aspect of traditional church life that some people might worry about losing. Human beings generally enjoy ritual, and we do it so well in church, whether it's the ritual of a solemn preparation for the Eucharist or the arrangement of biscuits, sugar and milk jug for the Enjoyment of Coffee afterwards. In fact, as we have already reflected wryly, an action done more than once in a religious setting runs the risk of becoming a ritual enshrined for all time. There is the story (can it be true?) of a missionary who went back years later to visit a church he had helped to establish in a hot country. He asked afterwards, 'What was the meaning of that strange action that the priest did with his hand during the service—a sort of flapping from the wrist in front of his face?' 'Oh, it's part of the ceremony,' came the reply. 'I don't know why we do it—we have always done it.' It was only later that the missionary remembered one of the earliest services he had led for the church, when a particularly irritating fly had kept buzzing round his face...

Meaningless ritual aside, however, a rite or practised action can be a tool to help people participate in something that might otherwise be hard to understand. Take, for example, the intercessory prayers. Here's an example of the same prayer activity, ostensibly suitable for all ages, carried out in two different styles.

Style One

'So have a bit of coloured wool—just snap off a piece from the balls of wool I'm leaving at the end of the rows. You'll need four bits in different colours, one for the world, one for the church, one for someone who's ill and one for something else on your mind at the moment. You choose which colour's what. Oh, I've forgotten to bring any red.

Never mind. Make that three prayers. Then, when you've prayed your prayer that goes with each colour, go and shove it in this plastic bag that I'll put... Oh, tell you what, I'll get a table out... George, could you find me a table from the hall to put the bag on? OK, everyone, get praying, then.'

Style Two

'Inside your service sheet today there are three strands of coloured wool. We're going to use these to help us pray for the world, the Church and people who are ill. So take the green piece—which is green like the land on a map— and, while the music plays, bring a particular country or place quietly in your heart before God, tying the green on to the red piece. Then take the red piece—red like love hearts—and pray for the Church. You might like to pray for our mission link in the Gambia, too. Tie the red on to the yellow piece. Then take the yellow piece—which is pale like someone who's feeling ill—and pray for anyone you know who is ill. When you've finished, bring your prayer strands, fastened together like this, and tie them on to the cross to show that you're placing your prayers in Jesus' hands. When everyone's brought up their prayers, I'll lead us in the Grace. Let's pray.'

It's exactly the same activity, led in two very different ways, one very much informal, the other with an air of ritual. Ritual gives a dignity and symbolic weight to activities. It can elevate their significance and provide the bridge between earth and heaven, the ordinary and the numinous. It's dangerous to fall into a trap of thinking that ritual means stodgy and meaningless, or that informality means easy access to God and an excuse not to prepare properly. In many cases, the more informal you want to appear, the better your stage management needs to be, like a host entertaining guests apparently effortlessly by dint of attention to minute detail beforehand. In a production of the play *Shakers* by Jane Thornton and John Godber, the hardest part for us as actors to rehearse and perform was the apparently random movement of four cocktail waitresses around a busy bar area: it took an incredible amount of attention to the detail of timing and speed. It could only look as spontaneous as it did because we knew to the half-second whose plate of pasta was being whisked in front of which strangely-named cocktail while someone else's birthday cake was being carried downstage.

Leaving aside the small number of people who will refuse to join in anything at all, most will feel safe to participate in an activity that has clearly marked boundaries. In the prayer activity above, it might seem dictatorial to tell people what each colour of wool represents, but, if half their time is spent worrying that they haven't remembered the three areas to pray about, and which colour should be which, that means they lose half their praying time. Also, if they're not sure what is the 'right' thing to do, they're unlikely to risk getting out of their seats to be shown up as getting it wrong. I certainly wouldn't!

Ritual is also reflected in the equipment we use. If we are going to use objects (paper, Post-it notes, empty bottles, candles—whatever they may be), let's give these 'modern' objects the same weight and dignity that we grant to the more traditionally 'sacred' objects in a church—the candlesticks and Communion cups that we lock away in the safe. If a Post-it note is carrying the prayers of the people to God, is it any less important than a thurible? Let's think through the ritual and make sure the experience is reassuringly well-prepared: the examples above illustrate the need for properly cut strands of wool, an appropriate receptacle for the wool and a suitable placement for the receptacle. A scruffy carrier bag on a table might be an appropriate container for prayers that are deliberately centred on litter or consumerism or the throwaway nature of society, but there is no excuse if it's simply the first thing that comes to hand: it hardly invests our prayers with significance.

Ritual, seen as good stage management and effective leadership, is a valuable tool for all-age worship. It sets people free to understand the meaning of worship, rather than leaving them floundering in the mechanics of how they go about doing it.

In this context, we should also remember that many leaders worry about having to be new and different every single week if they're doing all-age worship. In fact, a good framework for a service involves everyone knowing roughly how long it will be, with a mixture of the comfortingly familiar and the challengingly different. This kind of framework can stay the same for a length of time—a month, a term, a year or whatever you know to be appropriate in your situation. It can be positively unhelpful to do something radically different and unpredictable every time, besides being unsustainably exhausting. Also, if you've taken the time to learn a particular technique—a simple drama activity like hot-seating, a way of praying, the words of a prayer or response, or even something purely mechanical like a way of dividing into groups—it makes sense to reuse the technique and make the most of the time invested in teaching it. It's only when your framework runs the risk of becoming stale and clichéd that worship should be transformed and renewed. 'Change for the sake of change' is a dangerous road to walk, just as is 'staying the same because we've always done it like this'.

Adrenalin

Hope Hamilton Church, featured on the Fresh Expressions website and the second *Fresh Expressions* DVD, have gone right outside the boundaries of traditional church. On Sunday afternoons, their church 'Adrenalin' meets. They set out to a piece of recreation ground nearby, set up a barbecue, untangle the kite strings and another time of worship begins. Gradually, others arrive, play on the basketball court, have their nails painted, fly kites or simply chat. A story from the Bible might be included, and the time finishes with a prayer. It's a time for getting to know the neighbours and for the church to be visible in the community. The minister believes that there are more creative models of being church than simply gathering in a dedicated building on a Sunday morning: 'Our aim is to provide an opportunity for people to have fun together as church... where life, fun, outdoor pursuits and faith interact.'[21]

Adrenalin church members have decided on a time and place accessible to all ages; their activities can be enjoyed by all ages; there is time and space for relationship-building and for modelling worship across the age groups. People might well be encouraged or discouraged to attend because of the style of activities the church has chosen to enjoy together, but they won't be put off because they are too young or too old.

Conclusion

Coping with change can be very tough for people in established churches. There can be a mindset which dictates that our services should never change from how they were run in our childhood, even if that was 90 years ago—because that reflects the unchangeableness of God. We need the graciousness that comes from deep and strong relationships in order to help each other to worship in the best way we can offer God. Sometimes we need to let go and create a new congregation alongside an existing one, but the need for mutual graciousness then becomes greater than ever as we seek to learn from each other, not to compete. One of the interesting developments of Messy Church has been the way we have discovered and rediscovered truths that can enrich our established churches, if there is an atmosphere of trust and a willingness to listen. Both longer-established and newer churches have so much to learn from each other to further the kingdom of God and to make disciples. Let's do everything we can, from both sides, to build mutual trust, respect and openness so that we don't get in the way of what God is doing at this exciting point in history.

*

– Chapter 6 –

Planning an all-age service

We've thought about the theory and considered handling change, but how do we go about actually planning an all-age service? What elements come together in an all-age service?

On training days exploring all-age worship, the *Barnabas* children's ministry team sometimes use a short, almost-rhyming mnemonic to sum up the different touchstones for all-age worship:

short, simple
senses, symbol
space, imagination
pattern, participation

We have looked at some of these aspects in detail in Chapter 4 and have implied their existence throughout the book, but let's summarise here as a reminder.

- **Short:** most people don't have the attention span of an academic audience accustomed to one-hour lectures. The whole service should be short: Messy Church fits a lot into 15 minutes; another local church has no longer than 45 minutes for its Sunday service. Let everyone know how long the service will be and stick to it. Each element of the service should be short. Length does not make a prayer, reading, talk or entire service holier. Church isn't an endurance test. We should always leave them crying out for more.

- **Simple**: one clear message, reiterated in different ways through different media, is more effective than trying to celebrate the whole Christian story with all its ramifications in every single service. Using simple means to celebrate God is better than complicated, gimmicky visuals and effects that leave you overawed but unable to remember quite why the pyramid of melons, for example, was so important. Remember that simple language is not the same as childish language.

- **Senses**: we worship with the whole of ourselves, not just our cognitive faculties, so, as a general guideline, try to include the use of two senses in each activity. Senses also link our worship to the rest of our lives outside church, because we are using those senses and feeling those emotions in school, home or work. In church we have the opportunity to see how these vivid parts of our personalities fit into the larger framework of faith.

- **Symbol**: symbols are accessible by people at all levels of understanding and age and can be explored at different levels. The cross, bread, wine, fire, light, the dove, water, oil, trees, stones, honey, snakes: all are timeless symbols that can help us discover and rediscover truths about God through worship. They can be appreciated just as well by a child as by a learned professor—and the appreciation of a symbol by both these people can be enhanced by seeing it through the eyes of each other. One person needs to be reminded of the earthy reality of the object while another needs to have their eyes opened to its wider symbolism and where it recurs in scripture and in church life.

• **Space:** a church service may be the only time in the week when people are given the opportunity to be silent, to enjoy silence and to have deliberate growing space, so frame some quiet moments within the service with music, art or guidance in prayer or meditation. With all ages present, it's good to be realistic in our expectations of how long someone with a limited concentration span can be completely silent, be that a young person or an elderly one. It's also a good idea to help everyone to enjoy the vitality of communal moments of quiet, and not to expect to achieve the total silence that we might experience when alone.

• **Imagination:** make space for awe and wonder, for 'what if?' questions, for steps into the unknown, and for engagement with the numinous. Formulating good questions is more a part of discipleship than simply trying to learn the right answers. Use story, music, art, drama and dance to cross over into mystery. Avoid the temptation to explain everything and label everything. Share God's story as it is happening in the lives of the church members: testimonies and answers to prayer are important to celebrate together. Keep alive the imaginative link between what happens in a church service and what happens in the rest of our lives at home, school and work.

• **Pattern:** don't try to be radically different every day/week/ month. We all need rhythm, pattern and routine, with familiar things to rediscover as well as new ones to explore. Enjoy ritual and liturgy when it springs from the heart of the people and not from a lack of imagination for finding anything better. Make the most of the freedom to shape a pattern that is right for your particular place, time and people. Consider using the church year as a tool to colour worship and vary the pattern.

• **Participation**: consider your church members as protagonists, not spectators. Remember that people of all ages may want to be doing, taking part and joining in, not just watching and listening. Children may not be the only ones whose preferred learning style is active!

Putting together an all-age service

Assemble a team of people with a variety of gifts, outlooks and ages, at a time of day when everyone can make it. A good number to work with is between four and six. If nothing else, the presence of team members under the age of ten will ensure that you finish nice and early. (You will need to make sure that all adults in a leadership position in the presence of children are CRB-cleared and that good practice is observed as much at the planning meetings as on other occasions.)

Meet in a comfortable place with access to Bibles, a phone, big sheets of paper and the internet. ('There's a website on that. Let's find it now…') Have contact numbers of other church members to hand for speedy consultation: 'George would be good at that. Is he free that day?' 'I think Jackie has one of those. Can we check with her now?'

If possible, include a welcoming time to eat and drink together, even if it's something very simple. Remember to be imaginative in what you offer: tea and coffee may be appreciated by some, but juice and crisps may be preferred by others. Offering something that's a bit of a treat changes the tone from a working party to a proper party. Make sure everyone knows everyone else: shy people won't like to ask names and may have forgotten who everyone is since the last time you met.

If this is not the first event you have planned, spend some time reviewing and reflecting on the last service you arranged. A simple 'What went well? What could we improve on?' can take you a long way into learning from past experience.

When starting out, it's worth having a basic outline of a service order as a 'given' to work to. If everything is up for grabs, you might never make any decisions, and a blank sheet of paper is far too threatening for most groups. Plan on sticking to a set order of service for a given length of time—perhaps a term, six months or a year, depending on how often your all-age service occurs. Plan to review the service framework after that time and revise as necessary. A good time to try out one-off changes is at seasonal celebrations like Christmas, Easter or Harvest.

Begin by praying together in a way that includes everyone, giving them all a chance to pray out loud. Then let everyone know how long the planning meeting is going to last and make sure that you stick to that finishing time.

Turning to the next event, make sure everyone knows what the theme of the service is to be (ideally, they will know this before the meeting and will have had time to reflect on it). Bring people up to speed with any useful background information on the subject that they won't have accessed (from your supply of commentaries and Bible encyclopedias, for example).

Then have an 'anything goes' session when you simply jot

down every idea suggested, with no value judgments made on any of the suggestions, no matter how far-fetched. Move on to thinking about the component parts of the service. Write them out and fill each slot with a suggestion. Reflect on how well these ideas flow into each other and amend as necessary.

Consider allocating a personality profile to each member of the planning team (see the Appendix, pages 174–180) and use the profiles as touchstones to assess the suitability of each stage of the service. This will move you away from 'What do I like?' and into an understanding that we are here to serve God and each other. When the service has been planned, you might take turns to suggest how the person whose profile you have been given might respond to each element, and consider whether changes are needed as a result.

Make sure you decide who will take responsibility for preparing and leading each part of the service, or making sure it is prepared and led by someone else not on the planning team. Finally, end with a prayer activity led by a different person on the team each time (yes, *of course*, including the children). Prayers might include activities like passing round an object so that whoever holds it prays aloud or silently, finishing the prayer with 'Amen' and passing on the object to the person beside them. It could mean handing out objects that represent each part of the service and inviting different people to pray for the part of the service they are 'holding'. It could mean playing a team game of prayer noughts and crosses, with T and P instead of O and X: every 'T' that is placed down evokes a prayer of thanks, while every 'P' elicits a prayer that begins with 'please', from the team placing it down. The possibilities are endless.

If you have overall responsibility for what will happen,

remember that you retain the right of veto: you can hone the suggested service to perfection on your own later. Email or send round a copy of the service as soon as possible after the meeting, with the jobs clearly marked and a note of who is responsible for them.

Questions for the planning process

As you start out on your planning process, it is worth thinking through what you are trying to achieve in each part of the service. Thinking about why we do something can give us fresh inspiration for presenting it in a new way. As different church traditions will use the component parts of a service in different ways, the following questions are a general guideline rather than a template to follow rigidly. The one question that we must ask each time, under each heading, is, 'How can we encounter God?' That is the bottom line.

Welcome

- How can we signal the start of the service?
- How can we help everyone to feel that they are welcome and matter?
- How can we remind everyone why we're here?
- What else is the opening of a service trying to do?

Confession

- How can we give people the opportunity to know God's forgiveness and to make a fresh start?
- What else are we trying to do through a confession?

Music

- How can we help everyone to celebrate God's love?
- How can we introduce, explore and respond to the theme of the service through song?
- What else are we trying to do through music?

Exploring God's word

- How can we bring God's word to life?
- How can we hear its challenge and/or comfort?
- How can we let it change us in our everyday lives?
- How can we encourage a lifelong love of God's word?
- What else are we trying to do through exploring God's word?

Declaring what we believe / the 'creed'

- How can we remind ourselves of the big story of the Christian faith?
- What else are we trying to do through this declaration?

Testimony

- How can we witness to what God is doing today?
- How can we celebrate what he's doing in the lives of our community?
- What else are we trying to do through sharing our stories?

The Lord's Supper / Communion

- How can we remind people of Jesus' death and resurrection?
- How can we grow more unified as a body through the bread and wine?
- What else are we trying to do through the Lord's Supper?

Prayer

- How can we bring before God the needs of the world?
- How can we learn key prayers (such as the Lord's Prayer)?
- What else are we trying to do through prayer?

Blessing

- How can we best pray for God's blessing on everyone?
- How can we help everyone know that they have received God's blessing?
- What else are we trying to do through a blessing?

Notices

- How can we ensure everyone knows what's going on in the life of the community?
- What else are the notices trying to do?

Ending

- How can we signal the end of the service?
- What else are we trying to do through the ending?

When you have decided on the different parts of the service, you may occasionally want to use one of these tables to check whether you're leaving out any particular group of people, especially if you have a small congregation. Don't try to use them all every time—it would be a sure-fire route to madness. Note: you will see that there isn't a table for different age groups: please don't create one!

Have we included elements that appeal to people with different learning styles?

Part of service	Visual learners	Audio learners	Kinaesthetic learners	Sense-based learners	Discussion-based learners	Reading-based learners

Have we included elements that ensure we are worshipping with our whole selves?

Part of service	Sight	Sound	Touch	Taste / Smell	Cognition	Emotion	Imagination

Have we included elements that provide for a variety of responses to God?

Part of service	Loud	Quiet	Silent

Have we included elements that will help all of us along our discipleship path, whatever our stage of faith?

Part of service	People who have not yet made a commitment of faith	People who feel they belong to the faith community	People who are questioning and searching	People who have a mature faith

Content-wise, have we included celebrations and explorations of the different ways in which God acts?

Part of service	God's actions in history	God's actions in the lives of Christians in other parts of the world	God's actions in the lives of Christians from our gathered community

All-age service plans

Here are three examples of all-age service plans to help you start thinking about different possible shapes for your own worship services. There is a service of the word (a service whose focus is on the Bible-based talk or sermon), a story-based service and one that builds on different learning styles. The italicised sentences are a 'running commentary' on the aims in each part of the services.

An all-age service on the theme of thankfulness to God

We want to enable people to encounter God through a spirit of thankfulness, remind people why we should be thankful to God and express our thanks to God in different ways.

Welcome

We want to introduce the theme of thankfulness by building on people's own experience of saying 'thank you'. We want everyone to feel included and to know that they matter.

Thank people for coming today.

Invite everyone to think of something they would like to thank the person next to them for: making them breakfast in bed, perhaps. If they're next to someone they don't know, perhaps they could say, 'Thank you for smiling at me when I sat down in this seat' or 'Thank you for wearing a colour that cheers me up.'

Take a moment to say 'thank you' to each other and then tell everyone that 'thank you' is the theme of today's service.

We want to provide some visual reminders of the theme and demonstrate that we are all involved in the worship.

Ask for volunteers to help. They will bring up a bunch of flowers, a box of chocolates, a thank you card or a bottle of wine to place on the table during the song.

Song

Say, 'These are ways we might say "thank you" to someone who has done something for us. We're gathered here today to say "thank you" to God. We won't be giving him flowers and chocolates, but we will be finding out more about how to thank him.'

Confession

We want to explore the way that we forget and omit to give thanks to God. We want to remind people of the need to be humble and contrite before God. We want to hear voices other than the main leader's.

Before the service, ask two people to prepare a very short drama in which one person loads another down with presents. The one receiving the gifts never says 'thank you', just demands more and more, while the giver gets sadder and more upset. Present the sketch at this point in the service.

Alternative: read out a dramatised version of the parable of the Pharisee and the tax collector (Luke 18:9–14). You could simply have the different parts read out by a narrator and the two main characters; or you could read out the parts but have it mimed as it is read; or you could use a version like the one in *The Gospels Unplugged*.[22] The reading could be performed spontaneously or prepared in a very short rehearsal period beforehand.

We want visual links with the world outside the church meeting room.

Say, 'God has given us so much! Let's take a moment to think of all the wonderful gifts that we sometimes take for granted…'

Show projected images of food, a house, someone giving a hug, something beautiful from nature, clean water, people worshipping in freedom, toys and gadgets and appliances, a police officer to represent law and order.

We want a chance to join our voice to others'.

These lines could be read by different people with everyone invited to join in the response: 'We're sorry. Please forgive us.'

Dear God, you give us so many gifts. When we forget to say 'thank you'…
Response

You give us food, friendships and families. When we forget to say 'thank you'…
Response

You give us freedom, security and shelter. When we forget to say 'thank you'…
Response

You give us a hope and a future. When we forget to say 'thank you'…
Response

You gave us your own Son, Jesus. When we forget to say 'thank you'…
Response

Dear God, who gives and forgives, thank you for your forgiveness that you give so generously. Help us today to make a new start and to live our lives as your grateful people.

Songs of thankfulness

We want to thank God in a variety of ways, including loudly!

Exploring God's word

We want to meet God through his word, the Bible, and enter imaginatively into the feelings of the people we hear about in it. We want to understand what the passage is about and apply it to our own lives. We want a chance to respond to the passage and to air our questions.

Ask if anyone has ever given a present and the person has taken it without saying 'thank you'. How did the giver feel?

Ask for eleven volunteers to come and do an unrehearsed mime to the reading—Jesus and the healing of the ten lepers (Luke 17:11–19). Read out the story and briefly give any necessary background information, such as what leprosy is and the Jewish customs surrounding the treatment of people with the disease.

Hot-seat a volunteer playing the part of the man who said

'thank you' and another volunteer playing one of the men who didn't. This can usually be done spontaneously but the volunteers could be forewarned, especially if they are expected to 'perform' in front of large numbers of people.

Ask everyone to discuss in small groups how Jesus might have felt when the one man came back to say 'thank you'.

Say: 'None of us may have been healed of leprosy, but Jesus has done so much for us. Thankfulness is not just an action but a state of mind which remembers that everything comes from God and that we rely on him for everything. This means that we give thanks even when we don't feel like it, because it shows that underneath we trust him for everything. It's the opposite of self-reliance and arrogance. Our God isn't a machine but a person who longs for us to be in a relationship with him. We wouldn't say "thank you" to a slot machine, but we do say "thank you" to a person.'

Prayer

We want to meet God through prayer inspired by the passage. We want to bring before him the needs of the world.

Show a big picture of the man healed of leprosy kneeling at Jesus' feet, either drawn by someone in your congregation or found by searching 'images' on the internet. Have pens and speech bubbles on sticky notes available for each set of seats.

Say: 'Imagine this is you kneeling at Jesus' feet. What are you particularly thankful to God for? We also need to pray for other people and places in the world, so we'll put our "please" prayers on this picture too. In groups, help each other to draw or write your prayers. "Thank you" prayers go in yellow speech bubbles; "please" prayers go in green speech bubbles. When you've written or drawn your prayers, send a member of your group to come and stick your prayers on the picture. We'll bring the picture into the hall afterwards so that everyone can read the prayers.'

Play some quiet music from a CD while the prayers are being prayed. (Live music is another option, of course, but means your musicians can't join in the prayers.)

We want to pray one of the greatest prayers of the Christian faith.

When all the thank yous and pleases are stuck on the picture, comment on what you have created between you. Ask some volunteers to place the chocolates, flowers, card and wine around the picture as a symbol of different ways of thanking, and draw all the prayers together in the Lord's Prayer—a prayer that acknowledges God's love, his provision and his forgiveness.

Blessing

We want to meet God through a declaration of his blessing. We want some uplifting words that fire our imaginations.

Say: 'You might like to hold your arms open wide to receive God's blessing, like receiving a huge present from him.

'Even if our hands were as wide as the world and our arms could reach to the far side of the stars, we would still not be able to hold a thousandth part of all the blessings you give us, generous God. Bless your people now. And help us, like the man who was healed, to "get up and go" out to your world, in the love of Father, Son and Holy Spirit.'

Final response

We want to extend the influence of the service into the week ahead and provide an impetus to talk about God at home.

Invite everyone to take home a copy of a psalm that needs finishing and to bring their finished psalm back next week to become part of the thanksgiving in the service. They could even work on their version of the psalm with other people in their neighbourhood or home. This version is based on Psalm 103.

Thank the Lord.. *[your name]*

All that I am—my .... ,
my ....—praise his holy name.
(What can you praise God with?)

Thank the Lord, ..., *[your name again in case you've forgotten]* and don't forget all the good things he has done for you:
Like ....
and ....
and ....
and ....
(What big things has he done for you that you want to thank him for?)

I thank you for the way you've worked in the life of ....
....
(Who do you know who has met God?) and for the things you've done for them: ....
(What has he done for them or through them?)

I thank you for being so ....
and..
and .... *(What is God like?)*
You are slow to .... and full of
....
You never .... but you
always ....

I thank you for showing your love to me by giving me ....
....
and ....
and ....
(What else has God done in your life?)
You see? The Lord is like a .... to me!

Compared with God's everlastingness, I am like ....
....
But God's love for me goes on as long as ....
....

Thank God, you ....!
Thank God, you ....!
Thank God, you ....!
(Which individuals or groups, people or places or creatures will you call on to praise God with you?)

.... *[your name again]*, thank God!

Ending

We want to signal the end of the service and invite everyone to stay and chat.

Say: 'As we end our service and have a drink together, let's see if we can thank God for himself, for each other and for the week ahead of us. We'll say "thank you" five times, starting off as quietly as we can, By the time we get to the fifth "thank you", we'll be shouting as loudly as we can...'

Thank you... thank you... thank you... thank you... THANK YOU! Amen!

A story-based service based on the parable of the prodigal son

This service is shaped by the structure and events of Luke 15:11–32, inspired partly by Bob Hartman's approach to story-based services. He includes twelve outlines in his book *All-Age Services*.[23] The attractive aspect of this approach is that everyone can live the story and enter into it in a very personal way; it also takes the whole church on a journey of shared experience and automatically varies the structure of the service, giving it an element of excitement and unpredictability. The risk of this approach is that it can become very episodic and disjointed, so a good storyteller is needed to pull everyone together at each point. The storyteller could be someone different each time (young or old) or one person (not the service leader), to provide a change of voice and to make clear what is story and what is response to the elements of the story. Much care must be taken over the smooth transitions between activities.

If there is a suitable number of people and enough room, the service could move to a different place around the building for each part of the story, starting and finishing at the same point. This would represent the journey of the parable.

On the farm

We want to celebrate our lives with God and our gathering with his community of believers.

Storyteller: Jesus told a parable about a famer who had two sons. It wasn't a fairy-story family where everything was perfect, but they lived together on the farm and all worked together. The sons could be with their dad all the time and learn from him how to work the farm for the good of all the people who bought their food in the nearby market. The farm was a rich place, a warm place, a happy place that fed everyone round about.

Leader: We're here today to celebrate being close to our Father God and to celebrate the way we belong to each other. Let's pass round this fruit and enjoy a few moments catching up with each other and welcoming anyone we don't recognise.'

The leader gives plates of fruit to willing fruit-bearers, who offer them round to the congregation.

Leader: Now let's sing as a sign of celebration of being with our Father God.

Song

The younger son leaves home

We want to explore the theme of wanting to live life to the full and to feel what the Father might have felt. We want to place our hopes and dreams in God's hands.

Storyteller: So all was well on the farm until one day when the younger son came to his dad and said, 'Dad, I can't wait for you to die. I want my share of the inheritance now. Give me what will be mine when you die.' And the father divided his property between his two sons. Some time afterwards, the younger son took his share of the money and left home.'

Leader: The younger son longed for freedom and for adventure. He wanted to live life to the full. Jesus said, 'I have come so that you may have life—life in all its fullness.' What are your dreams? Tell the person next to you what you long for with your whole heart. Or tell them what you wish you'd done when you had the chance.

I wonder how the father felt as his son left. How does it feel when your children leave home? We're now going to hear from a member of our church who has had a similar experience.

A church member who has been asked beforehand describes how it felt when their child left home.

Leader: Let's take a moment to place our hopes and dreams and losses and bereavements in God's hands while we listen to this short piece of music.

Choose a short piece of instrumental music or an excerpt from a song expressing loss, from either a secular or a Christian source (for example, a section from The Fray: 'How to Save a Life' or Mahler's *Kindertotenlieder*).

From the city to the pigs

We want to bring our brokenness to God. We want to feel that we're not alone in our brokenness. We want to pray for those who are suffering in the world.

Storyteller: The younger son had a fantastic time in the capital city of a faraway land, spending lots and making lots of new friends. But one day, a famine hit the land. The son's money ran out and he eventually had nothing left. The only job he could find was the worst one in the world for someone from his background. It was a job that no one else would do: he had to look after filthy pigs. He was starving and wanted to eat the slops that the pigs were fed on, but no one gave him anything. One day he came to his senses and wondered what he was doing with his life. 'I know,' he said to himself, 'I'll go back to my dad and say sorry and maybe Dad will let me work for him again.' And he left the pig farm and set out on the long journey home.

Have a tray of broken eggshells; invite everyone to pick up a piece and to hold it.

Leader: Sometimes we make bad choices or everything goes wrong around us. Sometimes we just get in a bit of a mess. Sometimes we end up at rock bottom, broken and battered, just like these eggshells. We sometimes have a choice. We can either stay there, like the son in the pigsty, or we can choose to turn our back on our mistake and head back towards the person we love and the way of life we know is the best one.

As we hold these pieces of broken eggshell, let's pray out loud or in the quiet of our hearts for people known to us and those we hear about in the news who may feel fragile, broken and battered, or stuck somewhere they don't want to be, like the son was.

The son returns

We want to celebrate the God who runs to meet us in Jesus to bring us home.

Storyteller: The son was still a long way off from home when his dad ran out to meet him. The son

<table>
<tr><td></td><td>tried to say sorry for all the mistakes he'd made, but his dad gave him a huge hug and brought him back to the farm, getting people to bring him clean clothes and fine jewellery. They all celebrated his return with a huge party!</td></tr>
<tr><td>Leader:</td><td>The brokenness was transformed into colour and music and dancing as the son was brought back home by his father. It wasn't what he deserved but it was what the father wanted to give him—the best thing for him, a new start, a new hope. Let's turn our broken eggshells into a bright, beautiful picture of the son's return. You can use dye or felt-tips or sequins and glue to make the pieces as party-like as you can, and stick them together on this background. While we do this, we're going to sing some celebration songs together.</td></tr>
</table>

Art activity while songs are sung or music is played

Have a table with a variety of craft and art materials set up at a point that everyone can reach. You will also need the extra unused bits of shell from earlier, in case some people work faster than others and want to add more pieces to the design. Have a simple outline of the father and son rejoicing together drawn on a background panel of thick card, and stick the decorated eggshell pieces on to it. It will be messy, but that's OK!

The older brother

We want to reflect on the need to be gracious. We want a quiet time to let the story speak to us.

Storyteller: But this happy ending isn't the end of the story. Everyone was partying except the older brother, who learned why there was a celebration happening and was so furious that he left the farm in a terrible mood. His father came out and listened to him rant: 'It's not fair! I've been working for you all this time and you've never let me have a party with my friends! And this layabout comes home after wasting your money and you throw a party for him. It's not fair!' And the father said, 'My son, you're always with me and everything I have is yours. But don't you see? We have to have a party because your brother was dead and now he's alive. He was lost but now he's found.'

Display a picture of the parable. The Mafa portrayal of the return of the prodigal gives an interesting global perspective, and the Rembrandt picture, as we have already mentioned, is a classic, but a search for images under 'return of the prodigal' will provide many others to choose from.

Leader: It can be very hard to celebrate other people's gifts and achievements, especially when we don't think they deserve to have anything good happen to them. But this parable shows us the older son left out in the cold, unable to join in the party unless he can let go of his grudges and self-righteousness and share the joy of the dad over this person who has come home.

Let's be quiet for a few moments as we look at this picture of the parable as one artist imagined it. Let's ask God to show us where we are in this story and hear what he wants to say to us through it.

Have a few moments' silence.

Leader: Let's tell each other, if we want to, what we feel God's saying to us through this parable.

Ending

We want to signal the end of the service. We want to know God's blessing on all of us.

Leader: Let's ask for God's blessing on each other as we go out into our homes and jobs and schools. Let's ask God to be with us as we dream dreams, take risks, make mistakes and share his love in the places he leads us to.

Let's say to each other—say after me:

From the happiest place you find to the saddest place you go through, may you always find the way back home. And may you know the love of your heavenly Father as he runs to meet you in his Son, Jesus.

A service based on different learning styles on the theme of putting others first (Philippians 2:1–11)

Outline of service

- Breakfast
- Gathering
- Choice of response track
- Joint response to each other
- Joint response to God
- Prayer
- Ending

Breakfast

A staggered and leisurely start to the morning, giving everyone the chance to arrive over the course of an hour, to have either a full breakfast or just a drink and to build up community beforehand. You could have newspapers and simple games like Jenga, Battleships or Scrabble set out. (One Messy Church leader told me that the only reason one of the fathers in their congregation comes is because they provide the Sunday papers!)

It may also help to have posters with descriptions of the day's 'tracks' (as below) so that people can start to decide which one they would like to follow.

Gathering

At a set time, introduce the theme of the service and explain the possible options for the response time.

Hand out copies of Philippians 2:1–11 to everyone to write or draw on during the morning, or simply to have for reference.

Read the Bible passage. You might choose to have a simple reading, a dramatic reading with different voices reading different verses, a choral reading with different groups reading verses together, or the passage illustrated with slides or a single picture.

The leader shares information about the passage and its background, and any guidance as to how it might be relevant to your own church in particular. The leader then prays for God's presence with all the different tracks.

Choice of response track

I would recommend that no more than three of these should be available to choose from or the church will be swamped with indecision. Also, you would probably require too many leaders to run more than three effectively over a sustained period.

Each track requires one or more leaders: an individual, a couple, a group of friends or a family group might lead one. Ask parents to ensure that a responsible adult accompanies their child on the track they choose, or that the parent stays with the child. The session should last 20–30 minutes and each leader should be clear what time they need to draw the activity to a close.

You might feel as a church that, as a discipline, everyone should try every track at least once during the term/month/ year and not just head automatically for the one in which they feel most comfortable. If so, you may want to provide a system of remembering who has attended which track—

perhaps a register or stamp or sticker system to provide a framework for the learning. Remember that each track should be suitable for all ages, even the sermon and discussion.

- **Art track:** Create a piece of artwork as a response to the passage.

Leader: We're going to read this passage slowly out loud together twice. You might want to mark up your copy as we read it.

What words or phrases leap out at you? What do you think is the shape of the passage? What movement is there in it? What colours come to mind when you read it? What pictures do you get in your imagination? What do you think God is saying to us here today?

How can we together build these ideas into a picture?

Would anyone prefer to create their own individual piece of work based on the passage?

- **Talk track:** Help people who learn by listening.

A sermon: It's worth thinking about taking this group out of the main church building to another room, or adults may feel as if this is the 'proper' track to go to.

- **Discussion track:** Help people who learn by discussion.

Gather in a circle of chairs. Prepare your own all-age Bible study or use the following multi-purpose questions:

1. What excites you most about this passage?
2. What puzzles you most?
3. What is the biggest challenge in it?
4. What new thing have you learned about God from it?
5. What will you do differently this week as a result of reading this passage?

- **Practical track:** Respond to the passage in a hands-on, practical way.

The leader explains that this passage is about putting other people first and yourself last, just as Jesus did. To help the church do this, the group will build something for the ones who often get overlooked. Discuss why you have chosen a particular group—maybe children, teenagers, single people or the elderly—and set everyone to work making or doing what you have prepared for them. (You will need to estimate how much can be achieved in the time available; prepare well in advance so that the work can be finished on the day, or arrange for it to be finished elsewhere.) For example, the church toys for the preschool children might need washing and disinfecting, or a toy crate could be decorated. A bench might need an application of wood preservative to make it usable for the elderly. The teenagers' beanbags may need repairing. The cupboard belonging to one of the church groups may need to be tidied out. Tree branches may need trimming to aid access into parts of the churchyard.

This track could be extended to helping those in the wider community who are overlooked, with an activity that benefits them, like weeding the flowerbed of an elderly person in the neighbourhood or picking up the litter in the play area at the local field. You'll want to think about the health and safety issues of any of these activities, especially if you're including the elderly and the young.

- **Drama track:** Respond to the passage through drama, dance or music.

Given the time restraints, the leader will need to pre-plan an outcome: choreograph a dance or have the basic outline of a sketch worked out, or have the music ready for a song or piece of music to practise. Unless you have a peculiarly creative church, it's a very tall order to devise, rehearse and perform a piece from scratch. If you decide to use what you have prepared in the gathered worship after the track time, you may need to do some gentle ongoing teaching about the difference between worship and performance. But remember, some people come close to God through performance, too. Don't automatically create a 'show time': it can be even more valuable to work on something that is not a polished performance but simply an activity that helps the participants come near to God and to each other.

- **Silent track:** Be together but listening to God quietly.

Create a quiet space with candles, pictures relating to the theme, comfortable chairs, beanbags or kneelers, copies of the passage to write on, Bibles, pens, crayons, playdough, and the passage recorded on MP3 players or similar.

A leader introduces by explaining the equipment and how it can be used and sets the atmosphere by presenting guidelines: the group stays in the space together as they are on a journey together, but they remain silent to allow God to speak to them. After the set amount of time, they will have a moment to share (if they want to) what they have heard or experienced before they rejoin the rest of the church.

Joint response to each other

This is a time to come together as a church again and learn from the experiences of the other tracks. The joint response will need careful chairing on the part of the leader or it could take hours and destroy all the creative energy that has built up. Keep the emphasis on learning about God from each other, not on 'showing off'.

Joint response to God

This is a time to gather everything that has been experienced and offer it back to God as prayer. The time can expand to take in prayers for others in the world, other parts of the church and people who need God's touch. The prayer could be led in the style of a different track at each service. For example:

- **Art**: drawing prayers inside empty picture frames—one for looking to the interests of others, one for praising Jesus for all he has poured out for us, and one for people who haven't yet heard that Jesus is Lord—and placing the prayers next to a picture of Christ in majesty.
- **Talk**: spoken prayers with simple response phrases or 'Amen'.
- **Discussion**: talking about the prayer needs before praying for them informally, aloud and in no set order.
- **Practical**: short down-to-earth prayers based on observed needs in the local and global communities.

- **Drama/dance/music**: prayers using hand movements and music with minimal words.
- **Silent**: prayer stations to visit in silence.

Ending

The leader briefly sums up the worship and learning, invites everyone to seek God in the week ahead and gives a blessing.

Multiplex

Here's an example of an all-age service that happens every week with the help of a team of about 30. The church has provided a space where people can worship together while pursuing the style of worship that suits them best.

In Dorset, Easton Methodist Church offers a service with a choice between traditional worship in the sanctuary, Messy Church (creative adults and children exploring faith together), a meditative room (tackling the word of God in a quieter way), and the 'upper room' for the young and young at heart, with a lively bunch of enquiring teenagers and a self-service café open throughout.

Multiplex also incorporates a time when everyone comes together—a time for sharing news and testimony or the celebration of Communion. All these activities are held together by a unifying theme taken from the ecumenical resource *Roots*.

Families, in particular, have been attracted because of the options available for children and young people. Multiplex also encourages people to develop their gifts and ministries—hence the team of around 30 people who make it happen week after week. The original idea was to create an environment in which people coming to the church were more likely to stay because they saw a flexibility in worship that was inclusive.[24]

*

Conclusion

It's difficult to condense what we're discovering in the all-age worship field into a 'creed', but perhaps the 'manifesto' with which we began this book takes us a little way along the path for churches who believe in an all-age approach.

A manifesto for all-age church

We believe in God who created us for him and for each other.

We believe in Jesus who welcomes young and old without exception.

We believe in the Holy Spirit who transforms the life of all believers, young and old.

We believe in meeting God most intimately in the lives of those who are different from ourselves.

We believe in a church that reflects God, the three in one.

We believe we grow closer to Jesus as his disciples when we:
- worship God in a variety of ways, both familiar and different.
- worship in community as well as individually.
- worship in a way that encourages everyone to participate.
- worship in a way that both enriches and is enriched by our everyday life.
- worship God with all that we are.

Let's unpack this manifesto a little.

We believe in God who created us for him and for each other. The God of the Bible is one who sums up the Law and the Prophets in the command to 'love the Lord your God with all your heart and with all your soul and with all your strength and with all your mind', and 'love your neighbour as yourself' (Luke 10:27). We pour out our lives to God and to each other and, in doing so, incidentally find out how lovely we are.

We believe in Jesus who welcomes young and old without exception. Jesus refused to let adults stand in the way of the children receiving their blessing (Luke 18:15–17). On his way to heal a child, he stopped to tend to an older woman who needed him then and there (Luke 8:40–48). He treated everyone with equal respect.

We believe in the Holy Spirit who transforms the life of all believers, both young and old. The Church is starting to open its eyes to the spirituality of children as well as that of adults. We are coming to understand that God works from before our birth until after we die. God has a job for all believers to do, regardless of age.

We believe in meeting God most intimately in the lives of those who are different from ourselves. God's people through the Old Testament were continually challenged by meeting God in unexpected outsiders: the Israelite spies were helped by Rahab; Nehemiah was helped by King Artaxerxes; Nebuchadnezzar became a model believer. Jesus himself was amazed several times by outsiders: the woman from Samaria; the Roman centurion; the one foreign leper who returned to say 'thank you' for his healing. From the day of Pentecost onwards, God has sent his believers out to witness to those from different backgrounds. Throughout the New Testament we see the struggles of the early church to become the church for all, regardless of religious or ethnic background.

We believe in a church that reflects God, the three in one. Just as God has given us the picture of the Father, Son and Holy Spirit sitting, working, talking and eating together (for example in Revelation 5; Genesis 1; John 1; Genesis 18), so we, his church, should try to bring all people together in all our activities. In doing so, we show what God is like and demonstrate the unity between humans that Jesus came to bring (as Paul describes in Ephesians 1:10).

We believe we grow closer to Jesus as his disciples when we worship God in a variety of ways, both familiar and different. As worship is trying to please God, not ourselves, it makes sense to explore ways of worshipping him that don't always come easily to us, ways that more experienced Christians can teach us, ways that newer Christians find helpful. It is often in the uncomfortable times that we mysteriously find ourselves closest to God, like Jeremiah in his cistern, Joseph in his well, or Jonah in his fish.

We believe we grow closer to Jesus as his disciples when we worship in community as well as individually. While we need to have an active, independent faith so that we don't lose heart as soon as we are away from other Christians, we are also called to commit to a Christian community, which for most of us will be a church. God has chosen to build his kingdom through the gathered church, and Christians who are called to be separate from a regular worshipping community are the exception rather than the rule.

We believe we grow closer to Jesus as his disciples when we worship in a way that encourages everyone to participate. Worship that is going to be meaningful for people in a postmodern society has to take into consideration a prevalent suspicion of authority and the desire of most people to make their own choices. The days of rote learning—one person at the front dictating to others, who merely imbibe indiscriminately what they hear—have gone in schools and should have no place in our churches.

We believe we grow closer to Jesus as his disciples when we worship in a way that both enriches and is enriched by our everyday life. We can only worship 24/7 when we are reminded every week in our Christian communities of the ways God is working at home and at work—away from the gathered church as well as within it. God is relevant, active and present in the whole of our lives and, to avoid the trap of boxing him into Sundays, we must ensure that our services refer back to our everyday life. Praise and worship can come as a response to what we see and hear of God's actions in the classroom or on the factory floor, and the whole church can benefit from skills and attitudes that people learn in the world of work.

We believe we grow closer to Jesus as his disciples when we worship God with all that we are. We are fully human, not disembodied spirits. God has given us bodies, imaginations and feelings as well as intellect and voice, and every part of us can be used to worship him. If we fail to use particular parts of ourselves in worship, we risk not living life to the full, not being the people God made us to be. In short, we're missing out!

All-age worship is shorthand for something much more profound than a form of worship that appeals to all ages. It strikes at the very heart of what we are trying to do in our churches and challenges many of the preconceptions behind the style of church service that has developed over the last century. Yet worshipping with adults and children together is not something new and trendy; rather, it is an ancient skill that we are just beginning to rediscover in our individualistic Western culture. From the extended worshipping family of Abraham, through the all-encompassing welcome of Jesus to the 15th-century vision of Rublev with the three different persons of the Trinity at ease together, we hear the challenge to go against the secular norms of our culture and do all we can to recreate a church that glories in its abundant diversity. It is so challenging that it is not a course to be followed without much prayer, soul-searching and discussion from every member of a congregation. But I believe it is also the highest call for a church, the best way of being church, of reflecting who Jesus is and of healing the world. It is about being whole and wholesome and holy. Once we start looking at the church through 'all-age' lenses, it becomes very hard to see anything else as a realistic option for growing disciples and celebrating our wonderful, diverse, unified God together.

*

Appendix

Personality profile cards

The preferred learning styles included here are:

- Visual: enjoys learning by seeing.
- Active: enjoys learning by doing or making.
- Senses: enjoys learning by touch, taste or smell.
- Emotions: enjoys learning when the emotions are engaged.

The other learning styles are self-explanatory.

The 'experience of God' is necessarily brief and is simply an snapshot of that person's spiritual state. Volume preference indicates whether this person is most receptive when the input is loud or quiet. Reading age ranges between 0 and 15.

Name:	Annabel
Preferred learning style:	visual
Experience of God:	been on several Christian camps and prays often
Concentration span:	20 mins
Age:	10
Volume preference:	quiet
Reading age:	14

Name:	Ben
Preferred learning style:	active
Experience of God:	just become a Christian through Alpha
Concentration span:	5 mins
Age:	45
Volume preference:	loud
Reading age:	15

Name:	Catherine
Preferred learning style:	listening
Experience of God:	brought up in Christian family; church is habit
Concentration span:	limitless
Age:	78
Volume preference:	quiet but is losing hearing
Reading age:	15 but sight is failing

Name:	David
Preferred learning style:	listening
Experience of God:	reads Bible notes daily
Concentration span:	30 mins
Age:	34
Volume preference:	quiet
Reading age:	15

Name:	Ellie
Preferred learning style:	through art, emotion, music
Experience of God:	meditates regularly at yoga class
Concentration span:	45 mins
Age:	23
Volume preference:	any extreme
Reading age:	15

Name:	Frank
Preferred learning style:	active
Experience of God:	first time in church this week—came with wife
Concentration span:	3 mins
Age:	62
Volume preference:	loud
Reading age:	12

Name:	Gemma
Preferred learning style:	listening
Experience of God:	spent a lifetime questioning
Concentration span:	10 mins
Age:	19
Volume preference:	loud
Reading age:	12

Name:	Harry
Preferred learning style:	visual and active
Experience of God:	totally accepting
Concentration span:	30 secs
Age:	6 months
Volume preference:	quiet
Reading age:	0

Name:	Inez
Preferred learning style:	senses
Experience of God:	vivid and personal through family loss
Concentration span:	20 mins
Age:	55
Volume preference:	loud
Reading age:	15 (in Spanish; 6 in English)

Name:	Jim
Preferred learning style:	listening (especially stories)
Experience of God:	through Emmaus course
Concentration span:	5 mins
Age:	28
Volume preference:	quiet
Reading age:	15

Name:	Kate
Preferred learning style:	discussion
Experience of God:	conversion six years ago
Concentration span:	20 mins
Age:	17
Volume preference:	quiet
Reading age:	15

Name:	Liam
Preferred learning style:	visual
Experience of God:	meets him in every person, place and natural miracle
Concentration span:	1 minute
Age:	2
Volume preference:	loud
Reading age:	0

Name:	Mona
Preferred learning style:	taste
Experience of God:	intimate and joyful
Concentration span:	20 secs
Age:	33
Volume preference:	loud
Reading age:	0

Name:	Neil
Preferred learning style:	anything that challenges intellect
Experience of God:	been a Christian for ten years
Concentration span:	25 mins
Age:	36
Volume preference:	quiet
Reading age:	15

Name:	Olga
Preferred learning style:	reading
Experience of God:	through poetry
Concentration span:	1 hour
Age:	18
Volume preference:	quiet
Reading age:	15

Name:	Pete
Preferred learning style:	active
Experience of God:	close up and personal at Spring Harvest last year
Concentration span:	10 mins
Age:	89
Volume preference:	loud
Reading age:	13

Name:	Rebecca
Preferred learning style:	active, visual
Experience of God:	ever-present
Concentration span:	2 minutes
Age:	5
Volume preference:	quiet
Reading age:	5

Name:	Sam
Preferred learning style:	active
Experience of God:	none that he can articulate
Concentration span:	30 secs
Age:	8
Volume preference:	loud
Reading age:	6

Name:	Tammy
Preferred learning style:	discussion
Experience of God:	comes to church to see friends
Concentration span:	2 mins
Age:	14
Volume preference:	loud
Reading age:	12

Name:	Vince
Preferred learning style:	active
Experience of God:	leads house group
Concentration span:	5 mins
Age:	52
Volume preference:	quiet
Reading age:	15

Frequently Asked Questions

1. What is 'appropriate behaviour' in all-age services?

This question is sometimes code for 'Why can't children be quiet in church?' However, appropriate behaviour is more to do with whether or not someone is meeting God and helping others to meet him than with the amount of noise they are making. As far as I can make out, there's a three-way process: having a service that's engaging, having a congregation with godly priorities, and having parents who are trained and ready to help their children engage. Making the service as engaging as possible is useful, as we've been considering throughout this book. Helping the congregation to understand what's going on is important, so that they come to prefer having people in church making a noise rather than staying away for fear of upsetting others. It's equally important to equip parents or carers to know how to focus the service for their tinies, how to point out what's happening, what's important, what's fun, when to clap and when to be quiet.

It's worth remembering that adapting the behaviour of a group of people can take time, but that a gentle attitude of encouragement can change things more effectively than a critical, punitive approach. Any group of people learns to adjust to some sort of social rule that allows others to speak and listen, take turns, put others first in love and respect, give and take. Finding this social contract in an all-age service is less to do with 'what suits me' than with 'what suits the group'. It is too easy to say that a noisy child is 'behaving inappropriately'. If the child is bored and therefore noisy, perhaps it is the service that is inappropriate, and their response to it is actually entirely appropriate.

We need to provide services, model behaviour and invite people to participate in a way that puts others first. We need to help adults with children who are still finding their way in church by being an extended family, letting the joyous fact that those people are present far outweigh any temporary disturbance they may be making. A baby is screaming: does Mum feel happy to feed her or free to jiggle up and down with him at the back of church? A toddler is bashing a toy car on a seat: is there someone who can help her to bring herself and her car into the activity in which everyone else is taking part? A girl with special needs is waving and shouting: is the service paced so that there will soon be a change of scene or a change of activity? Is she met with disapproval or acceptance?

Behaviour is learned through modelling. Unconditional acceptance is learned through meeting it in others. It's obvious that if a new parent struggling with a toddler encounters disapproving looks and reprimands, they are unlikely to set foot in that church again. If they encounter smiles and thoughtful hospitality, they are much more likely to come back. I spent what felt like the first three years of my son's life gloomily sitting with him among toys in a cold belfry at the back of a medieval church: the only alternative was to stay at home, as the service could not cope with a bored toddler. Is that what I want for families who haven't yet got a strong commitment to a faith community?

2. Would you include pre-school children within the orbit of all-age worship?

Very definitely. Children at this age are absorbing impressions and truths faster than at any other stage in their development. Why take them out of their loving, worshipping family (and often remove them from their parent or expect the parent to be outside the gathered church) and then, in a few short years, have to teach them 'how to behave' in church? Members of the congregation need the powerless infant in their midst to remind them what Jesus was talking about when he said that we need to become like little children to enter the kingdom of heaven (Matthew 18:3). Change the building or the service to meet the needs of the families; don't break up families to meet the needs of the service. I would also encourage churches to persuade their children to sit with their families, not have 'all the children sitting on the floor at the front'. This latter course of action implies that the church is taking responsibility for the children's behaviour, and that's a very tall order when there's a service to run as well.

3. What about teenagers? What elements of all-age worship do we need to include in order to attract and keep them on board?

Can we really lump all teenagers together and assume they respond to the same things or meet God in the same ways, any more than we assume that all 70-year-olds must enjoy *Coronation Street* or singing war-time hits? What do we need to build in for teenagers (or for the middle-aged, children or the elderly)? Space to talk to them, listen to them, pray for them, mark what is important to them in a church setting, give them responsibility and recognise their gifts. Let's support them in their aspirations, recognise God in them and praise the good in them. Let's miss them when they're not there, weep with them when things go wrong, be there for them, challenge them, inspire them, always trust them, hope in them and love them even when they are at their least cooperative. What's best for their discipleship journey won't be marvellous programmes, great though these are; it will be acceptance and love.

4. How can all-age worship work with very large congregations?

A good sound system helps enormously! You also need to create spaces that allow people to be intimate within the larger crowd, and provide time to talk in pairs or groups, or to do an activity with people in the same row or at the same table. Enjoy the freedom that large groups give to be anonymous and loud. Movement and visibility may not be so easy with large numbers, so using projected images becomes more important. Rehearsal and 'stage management' also become crucial factors: moving ten people around a story-based service is a different matter from moving 150 people safely and speedily from one point to the next.

5. Can you suggest ways that all-age worship can work in pew-packed and column-filled church buildings, where movement and visibility are restricted?

As one who, at the age of eight, was horrified to hear that the vicar wanted to take the pews out of our village church ('But they've *always* been there!') I do understand the restrictions of some of the buildings in which we have to work. But if holiday clubs and church fairs can be run successfully in such buildings, let's not be daunted about running all-age services in them. Helping people to be as safe, comfortable, warm and dry as possible is a given; opening their eyes to the compensating beauty of the building in which it is their privilege to worship, reminding everyone of the Christians who have worshipped over centuries in that very place and giving the congregation ownership of that building are also important. At one all-age service I visited, families were encouraged not just to visit the hall and the foyer but to do activities in the main church building, even activities that included paint and glue. You might think about using the space imaginatively, not just sitting where you have always sat: side chapels and belfries have interesting atmospheres that could enhance different parts of the service or story you are exploring. (Which part of your church might represent Daniel's pit of lions or Elijah's cave?) If all else fails, there may be the option of holding your worship in a place that is more accessible—a hall or school or pub, for example.

6. How do we answer comments from many who feel that the teaching element of all-age worship must of necessity be 'dumbed-down'?

One approach would be to ask if the gathered church is always the best time for all cognitive learning to take place; whether we only learn through our cognitive faculties or whether there are other ways of learning and teaching that may be effective to help us meet God. There is also scope within an all-age service to have an accessible sermon or discussion as an option, as described in the service style 3 on pages 161–167.

7. How do you suggest we go about winning over those who are cautious or maybe even hostile to all-age worship?

Respect them and understand that what all-age worship aims to do flies in the face of what has been considered 'proper church' for many years in many denominations. I'm sure some Pharisees might have longed to follow the new way that

Jesus taught but were held back by a genuine fear of breaking God's law, which they loved. Similarly, some people have a sincere respect for the church traditions in which they have been brought up and find it hard to imagine that a different way of worshipping God can be acceptable. Introducing all-age services alongside traditional ones, not replacing the traditional ones, may be hard work but it gives people a chance to observe and to see their potential. Accept that what is irritating innovation at the start will, after two or three years, have become tradition, and people will be saying, 'But we've always shown DVD clips!' to your protests that you only bought the digital projector six months ago. It is also worth consistently teaching that the church should not exist for itself but for those who don't yet belong to it.

8. What evidence is there that all-age learning and worship are more effective than discipleship and teaching in homogeneous groupings?

Good question. I don't know that there is empirical evidence one way or the other. It would be hard to measure the effectiveness of one style of discipleship or worship over another. Certainly, Messy Churches are finding that the necessity of having a large team means that more gifts and ministries are recognised and exercised than might otherwise be the case. They are also finding that previously unchurched or dechurched families tend to stick with it—but it's all very new and difficult to assess objectively yet. The declining numbers of people in church over the last few decades implies that traditional church hasn't necessarily got the right answers either, of course. I would argue that unless the majority of people in a church congregation are wholeheartedly committed to all-age learning and worship, it is very hard to be effective in teaching, as adults tend to sit back and let the children 'do'. We must be intellectually committed to the all-age journey if it is to work.

9. People's worship tastes, music preferences and learning styles are so diverse. How can all-age worship and church hope to bring a congregation together?

By not pretending that we are all the same! All-age worship means confronting the notion that a 'one size fits all' approach on every occasion doesn't engage those who don't fit the average. We know we will be welcoming people into worship who approach God in very different ways and cannot be relied upon to hide their discomfort from the rest of the church, so we will try to make sure that the service is accessible and engaging to them throughout. There will always be give and take; any group of people trying to do roughly the same activity will have to wait their turn, make allowances, be humble and be gracious. Perhaps the difference with all-age worship is that this acceptance of diversity is built in, not hidden under a cloak of 'let's behave the same, whether we are engaged or not'.

10. What would you say are the key practical steps that a church can take to become a true all-age community, within which all-age worship can hope to take root?

Pray lots. Talk and listen lots. Check out the manifesto for all-age church (see p. 169) and the Child-Friendly Church scheme from Liverpool Diocese (from www.liverpoolchildstalk.co.uk) and discuss them at all levels of your church. Go to a service in your church and imagine that you are a child, teenager or elderly person: what would you want to change? Practise welcoming and hospitality at church and at home until it's second nature. Smile at everyone, whether or not you approve of what they're doing. Look for the good in people. Visit churches you have found by doing a search on the web (for example, "all-age service Wrigglington").

11. Where, either in church circles or in society in general, can I go to experience good practice of all-age worship and learning together?

Contact your diocesan children's adviser or equivalent in other denominations to ask for local examples of churches. Go to www.messychurch.org.uk to find a local example of this sort of all-age church in the directory. Read the stories from the Fresh Expressions website. Try sitting in some different types of restaurants and cafés and observing how at home different ages of intergenerational groups feel there. Theme parks are often advertised as 'family-friendly': when you next visit one, ask yourself if you would describe it as a truly all-age activity. Football matches often give a taste of a worshipping all-age community. Local authority establishments like craft centres and libraries often advertise workshops 'for all the family', so learn from these. Look at Christians in other cultures— for example, Asian, African, Chinese or Italian worshipping communities—to see how they behave together. Invite such a family round for a meal.

Useful books and websites

Philip Mountstephen and Kelly Martin, *Body Beautiful?* (Grove, 2004)

Jason Gardner, *Mend the Gap* (IVP, 2008)

Karen Marie Yust, *Real Kids, Real Faith* (Jossey-Bass, 2004)

Sue Palmer, *Toxic Childhood* (Orion, 2006)

Keith J. White, *The Growth of Love* (Barnabas, 2008)

Michele Guinness, *The Heavenly Party* (Monarch, 2007)

Leslie J. Francis and Jeff Astley, *Churches, Children and Christian Learning* (SPCK, 2002)

Richard Layard and Judy Dunn, *A Good Childhood* (Penguin, 2009)

Bob Hartman, *All-Age Services* (David C. Cook, 2009)

John Sutcliffe (ed.), *Tuesday's Child* (Christian Education Publications, 2001)

The All Age Service Annuals (Scripture Union, 2007/8)

Multi-sensory series (Scripture Union, various authors)

Lucy Moore, *Messy Church* (Barnabas, 2006)

Lucy Moore, *Messy Church 2* (Barnabas, 2008)

Nick Harding, *All Age Everything* (Kevin Mayhew, 2001)

Chris and John Leach, *How to Plan and Lead All-Age Worship* (Grove, 2008)

Nick Harding, *Boys, God and the Church* (Grove, 2008)

Chris Leach, *Keeping our Kids* (Grove, 2007)

www.messychurch.org.uk

www.barnabasinchurches.org.uk

www.familyfriendlychurches.org.uk

www.allageplus.org.uk

www.freshexpressions.org.uk

www.sanctus1.co.uk

www.rootsontheweb.com

www.northumbriacommunity.org

www.iona.org.uk

Notes

1   John Sutcliffe (ed.), *Tuesday's Child* (Christian Education Publications, 2001), p. 11.

2   Sutcliffe, *Tuesday's Child*, p. 28.

3   See Chapter 2 of *Body Beautiful?* by Philip Mountstephen and Kelly Martin (Grove, 2004). This explores the biblical background to all-age church, with an emphasis on the nature of God and the community of believers in the story of salvation.

4   Margaret Withers, 'All-age worship: a short review': www.barnabasinchurches.org.uk/2912

5   Mountstephen and Martin, *Body Beautiful?* p. 26.

6   Sue Palmer, *Toxic Childhood* (Orion, 2006), p. 157.

7   Richard Layard and Judy Dunn, *A Good Childhood* (Penguin, 2009), p. 151.

8   Jason Gardner, *Mend the Gap* (IVP, 2008), p. 167.

9   Mike Yaconelli, 'A better idea than youth ministry': http://wpcstudents.org. Click on Leadership - Leadership tools - Growth articles.

10 Keith J. White, *The Growth of Love* (Barnabas, 2008), p. 128.

11 Martyn Payne, 'Beware! Children's leaders at work': see www.barnabasinchurches.org.uk/3840.

12 You can find out about developments in Sanctus2nds by visiting www.sanctus1.co.uk.

13 See www.freshexpressions.co.uk/section.asp?id=2229.

14 Salley Vickers, *Miss Garnet's Angel* (HarperCollins, 2001)

15 White, *The Growth of Love*, p. 69.

16 Lucy Moore, 'House on the rock rap': www.barnabasinchurches.org.uk/784.

17 Jonathan Bartley, 'Children should be heard in church' (*Church Times*, 18 July 2008)

18 White, *The Growth of Love*, p. 68.

19 From www.northumbriacommunity.org.

20 Iona resources are published by Wild Goose Publications, available from bookshops or from www.ionabooks.com; Northumbria Community resources are available from www.northumbriacommunity.org.

21 Adapted with permission from the Fresh Expressions website.

22 Lucy Moore, *The Gospels Unplugged* (Barnabas, 2002), p. 27.

23 Bob Hartman, *All-Age Services* (David C Cook, 2009).

24 Adapted courtesy of Momentum (www.momentum-uk.org).